I Believe in God

Stuart D. Robertson

I Believe in God

ISBN: Softcover 978-1-951472-15-3

Copyright © 2018 by Stuart D. Robertson

All rights reserved. No part of this book may be reproduced or transmitted in any form or by any means, electronic or mechanical, including photocopying, recording, or by any information storage and retrieval system, without permission in writing from the publisher.

To order additional copies of this book, contact:

Parson's Porch Books

1-423-475-7308

www.parsonsporch.com

Parson's Porch Books is an imprint of **Parson's Porch & Book Publishers** in Cleveland, Tennessee, which has double focus. We focus on the needs of creative writers who need a professional publisher to get their work to market, **&** we also focus on the needs of others by sharing our profits with those who struggle in poverty to meet their basic needs of food, clothing, shelter and safety.

I Believe in God

Contents

Foreword 7
   Michael Bergmann

Introduction 11

I Believe in God 13
   Deuteronomy 6:1-9; Hebrews 1:1-6

God, the Father Almighty 26
   I Chronicles 28:1-6 Matthew 6:1-15

God, Creator of Heaven and Earth 34
   Genesis 1:1-13; Acts 17:22-31

I Believe in Jesus Christ, God's only Son 44
   Genesis 14:17-20; John 3:16-21

Jesus Christ, our Lord 55
   Isaiah 44:1-8; Acts 16:25-34

He was Conceived by the Holy Ghost, Born of the Virgin Mary .. 66
Isaiah 7:10-17; Luke 1:26-35

He Suffered under Pontius Pilate 72
   Isaiah 53:1-12; John 19:1-16

He Was Crucified, Dead, and Buried 79
   Psalm 69:1-21; Matthew 27:27-44

He Descended into Hell 87
   II Samuel 22:1-20 Ephesians 4:1-10

The Third Day He Rose Again from the Dead 94
   Job 19:23-27; Mark 16:1-8

Jesus Ascended into Heaven 100
   Isaiah 6:1-5; Acts 1:1-11

Jesus Sits at the Right Hand of God, the Father............................ 108
    Psalm 110; Mark 16: 9-20
From There He will Come to Judge of the Living and the Dead 114
    I Chronicles 16:28-36; II Timothy 4:1-8
I Believe in the Holy Spirit.. 122
    John 14:15-27
I Believe in the Holy Catholic Church... 130
    Deuteronomy 7:1-13; Matthew 16:13-19
I Believe in the Forgiveness of Sins... 169
    I Kings 8:33-40; Matthew 18:21-34
I Believe in the Resurrection of the Body 180
    Daniel 12:1-13; I Corinthians 15:12-26
I Believe in the Life Everlasting... 191
    Psalm 133; John 3:1-17

Foreword
Michael Bergmann

You have in your hands a book of sermons on the Apostles' Creed by Dr. Stuart Robertson, written and preached in late 1993 and early 1994 at Faith Presbyterian Church in West Lafayette, Indiana. I predict that as you read them, you will profit as I have from listening to him preach for many years when he was my pastor at this same church.

What style of sermon should you expect? What sort of a preacher is he? He's the kind of educated man whose education does not make him at all distant from others. He has a special interest in history, having studied (among other things) the ancient Jewish writer Josephus, whose work was the focus of his doctoral dissertation. In these sermons, you'll see occasional allusions to history, mostly to church history and Biblical history, but not limited to those. It's one of the places that his meditations naturally take him as he is reflecting on God, on scripture, on what we need to hear as we make our way through life, trying to follow in the footsteps of Christ. This is, I think, an especially helpful approach for a series of sermons on the Apostle's Creed, an historic document that has united Christians across many centuries.

Stuart is not a typical preacher of the late 20th and early 21st century. (His career as pastor at Faith Presbyterian Church, which wasn't his first pastorate, went from August of 1986 until he retired in April of 2007.) From him you won't get three-point teaching sermons. Instead, you get the unhurried careful ruminations of a thoughtful, kind, and devout man as he meditates on his theme for the week, on the words of scripture for that Lord's day, on the current needs and the perspective of his parishioners, and on what God wants from us. The flow of his sermons is more organic than it is structured with clearly delineated parts. It's like walking along a winding pathway in a forest, where you can't always tell what's around the next corner but are delighted or moved or challenged or illuminated by what you hear next, in ways that surprise you, that you didn't see coming.

In reading his sermons, you'll benefit from the kind of person he is: from his gentle manner, from his compassion for the needy who so capture God's attention, from his strong desire that he and his listeners will be of some use for good in the world, from his humility before God and God's word, and from his carefully crafted ways of speaking that reach out to people from all manner of backgrounds.

In taking in a sermon, one is taking in something of the preacher of the sermon as well. What you know of the preacher can affect what you hear (or read) and understand. To know the spirit of the preacher is to gain a kind of interpretive tool that can make the sermons more valuable and better appreciated. I can't give you a full picture of Stuart in a short foreword, but I'll try to give you a tiny glimpse of this unobtrusive but very winsome pastor, who is also a dear friend.

I've observed Stuart in many different contexts: in the pulpit at Faith Presbyterian Church, lecturing for a Jewish Studies audience at Purdue University, in church business meetings and prayer meetings, in light-hearted gatherings at church or in our homes or the homes of others, in reading groups, in the local work release jail where he has led Bible studies for many years, in times of joy and times of sorrow for him and for me. What I've seen repeatedly in the nearly two decades I've known him—in both his actions and in his words—are two things that I think make him a very attractive personality.

The first is that he's genuine. Pastors often feel that they need to act a certain way to fit their role. With Stuart, there is no acting, no phony religiosity. What you see is what he's really like. One thing I know he particularly hates is feeling pressured to act as if he's something he's not—especially when it comes to religious or spiritual matters. It's that complete genuineness—which I saw early on as he preached and in one-on-one meetings with him—that first drew me to him and made me want to go to his church.

The second thing that I think attracts people to him is the way he treats those around him with kindness and love. One example of this is the way he controls his tongue, speaking words that bring peace instead of words that increase tension. It's not as important to him to show that he's right or to clarify his position as it is to be careful not to say something unloving, the consequences of which he might come to regret. Another example is his tendency to see the good in people who think very differently than he does on religious matters. Whether they're from a different branch of Christendom or from some other religion or completely nonreligious, he can think very highly of them and to appreciate and admire the goodness in them.

A final example, perhaps the one that means the most to me, is the way he believes the best of people, expecting them to live honorably. I could see this in his conversations with children and young people and with people in the work release jail, when he led Bible studies there. By his words, he builds them up and helps them to feel that they can live a life that is pleasing to God. When I think of him in these settings, I am reminded of these words from Fred Rogers of the television show Mister Rogers' Neighborhood: "I believe that appreciation is a holy thing, that when we look for what's best in the person we happen to be with now, we're doing what God does. So, in loving and appreciating our neighbor, we're participating in something truly sacred." Watching Stuart interact with others is seeing that sacred and holy thing in action.

These two traits—his genuineness and his loving kindness—have characterized his life for all the years I've known him. They go a long way towards explaining why I and others very much enjoy his company. And knowing these things about him has enhanced my experience of listening to and re-reading his sermons. Perhaps your reading of these sermons will be likewise enriched by getting this brief look at the kind of person he is. I sincerely hope that in reading this book, you will benefit from his tutelage and wisdom as much as I have.

Michael Bergmann
Purdue University
Groundhog Day, 2018

Introduction

This book of reflections on the Apostles' Creed began as a series of sermons I offered at Faith Presbyterian Church, West Lafayette, Indiana in 1993. It is now a quarter century later. I retired from the pastoral ministry in 2007, after serving at Faith Church for twenty-one years.

After retirement I continued my work teaching a few courses in the Religious Studies Department and in the School of Languages and Cultures at Purdue University. I principally teach biblical Hebrew but also several lecture courses on early biblical interpretation as well as on the ancient Near East, the Israelites, and early Christianity.

I am aware how my experience as a lecturer in a public university has affected my thinking. It is not that my beliefs are altered. My convictions have not been reduced to hypotheses. Rather, whereas in my pastoral ministry I cared for a somewhat homogeneous congregation, I now do my work in an ideological mix. My associations now are with faculty, staff, and students that range widely from some very conservative and very progressive Christians, conservative and progressive Muslims, Hindus, Orthodox and Reform Jews. From the latter I learned of Abraham Heschel and Solomon Schechter, both of whom made an impact on me. Many of my students are at that time of life when they are unsure what they believe. Many of those with whom I mingle are friendly atheists, who like how I play tennis. That I was a pastor is seldom far from the background of our conversations.

What I have written in these reflections on the Apostles' Creed exhibits fruit from many of these conversations. In the process what were at first sermons have become a different kind of writing.

The purpose of reciting the Creeds is partly to remind ourselves that we are connected to the early Church. As they put it "we believe in the communion of saints." We are part of the Body of Christ that straddles time and continents. As we plunge on wordily in modern times, these succinct statements from yesteryear serve us well.

Each statement in the Creed draws on the Bible for its warrant. This warrant does not derive from proof-texts randomly selected but from the gist of the whole of Scripture. I will draw on texts within the Bible, all the while realizing that there are other texts that are not as clear or that differ. Within the Bible that includes writings brought together over centuries, there is development on key matters. As Robert Grant and David Tracy point out in their **A Short History of the Interpretation of the Bible**, p. 12-133, Jesus said once, "You have heard that it was said to the ancients 'Do not swear falsely' . . . But I say to you, 'Do not swear at all . . .'" (Matthew 5: 33); "and 'what they had heard" for the time was the word of God to them." The Old Testament command was not actually superseded as it was upgraded in a different time. The final version of the Bible's teaching, so to speak, is found in the Creed.

The purpose of this study is "practical" rather than "academic." For those that have had their curiosity stimulated by this focus on the Apostles' Creed, I recommend further reading in J.N.D. Kelly's book **The Creeds of Christendom** (1972**).** A book written by a Christian brother on the other side of the Tiber that has been of refreshment to me as I have tried to understand what is basic to our faith, is by the former Cardinal Joseph Ratzinger, **Introduction to Christianity** (2004). He is known better by his name after becoming Pope Benedict XVI.

Finally, I quote a hero of my childhood in India, Jim Corbett, who rescued many a frightened villager in India that despaired at life because of man eating tigers and leopards that patrolled the hills around Naini Tal. The winsome disclaimer in his book, **Jungle Lore** (Oxford UP, 1953) I would adopt as my own. "I do not flatter myself that all who read these pages will agree with my deductions and statements, but that need be no cause for quarrel between us, for no two or more people look at an object with the same eyes" (p. 57).

Stuart D. Robertson
Easter, 2018

I Believe in God
Deuteronomy 6:1-9; Hebrews 1:1-6

All around the world for the past sixteen hundred or so years if you were to ask a Christian what he/she believes, in a nutshell, the answer would begin, "I believe in God," followed by other details that mark the statement as specifically Christian.

These words that begin the Apostle's Creed have been for Christians very much like Deuteronomy 6:4-5 were for the ancient Jews and remain so. "Hear, O Israel: The Lord our God is one Lord ..." This is called the *shema*, that means "Hear!" It is the bed-rock of a Jew's faith, repeated morning and evening. However, the Jewish *shema* comes from the Bible, while the Creed reflects the attempt of the early Church to crystallize its basic beliefs based on the teachings of the Bible.

There are evident differences between these two basic statements. The *shema* begins with Moses' command to Israel, "Hear!" The Creed begins, "I believe." After the command to hear, *shema*, there is a confession of faith, "the Lord **our** God, **one Lord**." But then it goes on to give corollaries to the command to hear: "Love the Lord with all your heart, soul, and strength" and let the repetition of these words be constant among you and your families. The Creed, by contrast, proceeds to define the basic ideas a Christian is to believe.

Ancient Israel had another statement of faith that remembered God's care for them since the days of Abraham's grandson Jacob. This "creed" is found in Deuteronomy, 26: 5-10. When they brought their offering of first fruits of the harvest to the Lord they were to say these words, "A wandering Aramean was my father, and he went down to Egypt . . ." from which place God brought them out after being enslaved there. It was basic to an Israelite's identity to remember how they came to be a unique people. God's care for them from long ago remained pertinent to remember in every generation.

It might be thought that the Jewish *shema* and the second creed in Deuteronomy 26 focus on actions and the Christian creed on beliefs.

I have pondered this. But I wonder if in saying the two opening words, "I believe," the Christian is not walking in the footsteps of Abraham for whom believing God was demonstrated in what he did; he left home when God told him, "Go!"

The verses that follow the *shema* reveal how important it was in the Jewish people's life: "these words shall be upon your heart, and you shall teach them diligently to your children, and shall talk of them when you sit in your house, and when you walk by the way, and when you lie down, and when you rise. And you shall bind them as a sign upon your hand, and they shall be as frontlets between your eyes. And you shall write them on the doorposts of your house and on your gates."

The "Apostles' Creed," is a very old statement of faith but is not well known in all circles of Christianity today. The Nicene Creed is well known in the branches of Christendom that are liturgical in worship, but not in the large swath of Protestant Christianity that favors spontaneity over remembering its heritage. The Apostles' Creed played a crucially important role in my life.

The term "Apostles' Creed" was first used, of which there is any record, in a letter written in AD 390 by the Bishop of Milan, Ambrose, to the pope at the time, Siricius.

I was reared by missionary parents in India. "The Gospel" was my parents' stock in trade. It was for me the "ambient sound" in which I grew up. I went through the appropriate motions as a child that kept me in good stead with my parents and, they thought, with God, but all the words and ideas that percolated in the air I breathed never penetrated me. I believed enough to be scared that if "the second coming" happened I would be left behind because I had no idea how to believe.

Belief seemed to demand knowledge and visceral certainty. I had the former, but certainty never came to me. I knew the words expressing the "plan of salvation." I knew how to behave myself, and how to take my turn in saying "grace" before a meal, so my parents assumed I was a believer. And, of course, this meant the right kind of believer, the kind that was "like us."

My ennui in matters of faith came to a head toward the end of my first year of college. It was a scary moment in my life. This was no doubt in part because of the overall oddness I found trying to acclimate to life in America after growing up in India.

I tried to be a Christian, that is, to fit in to the little world of my parents and peers, but inwardly I was adrift. I was far from indifferent, but nothing clicked. Praying never worked. It was necessary but futile to pray. Praying for me was to repeat the words other people spoke when they prayed. "Dear heavenly Father, I just wanna thank you, etc." All these prayers accomplished was to make others think I was a Christian. It was denied to me to believe, to have faith.

So, for me the decision to leap out, to use a popular metaphor Kierkegaard taught us, to believe, that is, from the heart to begin to follow Jesus was big. It was a deliberate intention that I hoped would morph into inward certainty. It was an earthquake moment, a do or die attempt. There was no guarantee that this would evolve into the real thing, but it was all I could do. Having tried and failed to "believe" many times before, I tried again, very hard.

After the very traumatic period that followed this that compelled me to drop out of school, I attended a Presbyterian Church near the campus of the small Midwestern Presbyterian college in which I later enrolled. In that church I heard the Apostles' Creed. I'd never heard it before. I repeated it weekly. It infiltrated my memory. Slowly and surely it provided me an anchoring place. I avoided Sunday School because I was weary of the rehearsals of all the familiar ideas that never did anything for me. But I listened intently to the sermons of the kindly older pastor. I found the Lord's Supper emotionally moving. I would sit by myself in church on Communion Sunday because I would be unable to repress the emotions that overcame me; an embarrassing situation when nobody else appeared to be so affected.

Though my father was born and baptized into the Church of Scotland that had a heritage of orderly worship, my upbringing was in the kind of Protestantism he learned in this country that favored spontaneous "testimonies," and wasn't big into "formal," turns of phrase like the Creed. This was (or could become) "vain repetition," that Jesus warned against. I found, however, as I recited the Creed week after week, that it was sinking in.

Throughout my undergraduate years I adhered to a private life of trying to live out this leap into a way of life following Jesus. I wondered often if this was a mere decision like any other choice, or was there more to it than this? Was it just my choice, or was a deeper prompting at work in me?

Ask my roommates from those years, and they will tell you about my regular early morning rising for Bible reading and prayer—regardless of when I went to bed, and of my aloneness.

For me belief never came as easily as it seemed to come to most of my friends who were Christians. I dreaded and avoided Bible studies that brimmed with what seemed often rehearsals of self-confident and flippant truisms. Inwardly I wrestled a great deal as I kept up a regimen of Scripture reading, prayer, and self-examination of my "performance" as a Christian. Every day extended the lonely crisis of my decision.

When I got to graduate school, the shock of a new environment and the feeling of being more alone than I'd ever felt before seemed to act as an open drain-plug to my fledgling inward certainties. They just seeped away. It was fashionable among my graduate school colleagues to ridicule Christianity. The professor for whom I was a teaching assistant discovered that my faith was a matter of some importance to me, so he delighted to throw questions at me about Christianity, many of which I could not answer. But I kept on with my attempt to do what a Christian does—the Bible reading, the attempts to pray, and the more specific obedience having to do with attending worship, never missing the Eucharist, tithing my meager TA stipend, and trying to be helpful to other people.

Those years were so intensely painful for me that I often wondered if I was destined not to be able to believe anything at all. I feared having to make the decision that I could not believe after all and then to be compelled to live deliberately without faith in the God who somehow refused to give me any gift of inward certainty. I dreaded making this decision; I kept putting it off.

The reason why I spent two years studying the philosophy of religion at a seminary with an acclaimed faculty was that I needed more than anything else in life to find out if I could believe. How could I find belief? I never intended to become a pastor, but this stint in a seminary led to this, in a roundabout sort of way

Part of the problem I encountered that I think many people find, came from an idea of faith that crept into Reformed Protestantism early on after the break with Rome. Faith was not mere trust. The Heidelberg Catechism (1563) begins to define "true faith" this way: It is " not only a certain knowledge by which I accept as true all that God has revealed in his word . . ." True and "certain" are words subject to interpretation. But I understood true and "certain knowledge" as complete inward conviction of what was indisputably the factual foundation of right faith.

Cardinal Ratzinger wrote a very helpful comment on the parallel problems of the believer and the unbeliever. 'Just as the believer knows himself to be constantly threatened by unbelief, which he must experience as a constant temptation, so for the unbeliever faith remains a temptation and a threat to his apparently permanently closed world. In short, there is no escape from the dilemma of being a man'" (**Introduction to Christianity**, p. 45). The first chapter of this book is devoted to a penetrating examination of what constitutes belief and unbelief.

While it is true that in the Gospel of John we are taught to believe certain truths about Jesus as necessary, the exchange between Jesus and Nicodemas (John 3: 1-12) seems to make clear that belief in "being born from above" is not like knowledge of the ordinary kind. Nicodemus was no dummy. He was a "ruler of the Jews." Yet he did not understand the idea of "being born from above." No wonder. There was nothing like this in the Bible, that is, the Bible he and Jesus shared that was then only the Old Testament. We don't read in this Gospel passage that after Jesus explained "being born from above," it was an "eureka" moment for Nicodemus.

Jesus explained how this belief works: "The wind blows where it wills, and you hear the sound of it, but you don't know whence it comes or whither it goes; so, it is with everyone who is born of the Spirit" (John 3: 5). I can tell from which direction the wind blows, but I don't understand how winds start from scratch. We may rightfully apply this knowledge to the other aspects of Jesus' teaching that are also beyond the capacity of knowing as we know ordinary things. Did Nicodemus then say, "Oh, I get it now!"?

Though Jesus didn't refer to this as a mystery *per se*, it certainly is a mysterious teaching. Mystery is not alien to Christian teaching.

The word appears often in the New Testament; if I counted right, twenty-seven times. Jesus combined the word "know" with "mystery" in the Gospels ("unto you it is given to know the mystery of the kingdom of God" [Quoted in Matthew and Luke a bit differently than in Mark. I cite it as found in Mark 4: 11,] KJV). It suggests that the Kingdom of God is an intentional paradox—my term, but I think appropriate. The RSV translates the Greek word *musterion*, "secret." Among these places where mystery is used, I think it is used most sweepingly in the Apostle Paul's remark in I Corinthians 2: 7, "We speak the wisdom of God in a mystery." Here the RSV again avoids "mystery," but uses words also suggesting that the knowledge of the Gospel is unlike ordinary knowledge in referring to it as "secret and hidden wisdom of God decreed before the ages."

In the heat of theological battle of the Reformation, the word mystery smacked too much of the Church of Rome. So, the elusiveness of the things of God to ordinary understanding was promoted to a more definite kind of knowledge. To know (for certain) seemed to become a requirement for "true faith." In the process of this upgraded requirement a lot of thoughtful people were thrown for a loop.

Thus, the religious philosophy of the Reformers of the 16rh century became unlike both Jewish and Christian philosophy until that time. The great ninth century Jewish philosopher, Saadia Gaon, and the twelfth century Moses Maimonides recognized the tension between faith and reason. The Reformers found this tension inhospitable to true faith. Philosophy had become the "handmaiden of theology" long before in Christendom. Faith and reason aligned rather than remaining in tension. Reason became the argument that proved that what was believed was true, that is, virtually if not actually factual. This despite St. Augustine's awareness of the tension between faith and reason.

St. Augustine famously wrote: "I believe in order that I may understand." In this he seemed to me to take away the sting of having to prove matters of faith as one would make a mathematical proof or produce evidence in a court of law. He, like the Apostle Paul, knew that the mystery of the Gospel, that was the wisdom of God, was on a different order from the wisdom of this world.

In the twelfth century St. Anselm expanded on this, "I do not seek to understand in order that I may believe, but rather, I believe in order that I may understand." In this, I thought, there was no requirement for belief to be a certain knowledge. That is, unless by "certain kind of knowledge" you mean "a particular kind of knowledge," rather than absolute certainty.

In the training I received in philosophy of religion I discovered that "evidential apologetics" became the darling of the defenders of the Gospel. This kind of defense of the Gospel seemed to teach that you believed because you understood. So, the defense of the Gospel became an aggressive endeavor of debate to prove aspects of that growing "sphere" of the Gospel true. For many this sphere included believing the Bible was an infallible scientific and historical treatise, superseding "secular" science and ordinary history. The ramifications seemed to go on and on.

The enemy could be defeated by argument. What the Apostle Paul wrote, "Knowledge puffs up" (I Corinthians 8: 1), I found demonstrated as true, maybe particularly this kind of knowledge as portrayed by the aggressive debaters for the Gospel. Referring to the Bible as "God's Word," led to the need to defend it against the attacks of the "acids of modernity." It seemed to me an increasingly strange conceptual world.

The Bible's great love chapter's words meant little in this environment (I Corinthians 13), "If I have all knowledge . . . and have not love, I am nothing;" and "Our knowledge is imperfect;" and, "Now we know in part."

Such a recognition of how fragile our understanding of the mysterious things of God is does not contradict the urging of the Epistle of Jude, "Contend for the faith." Jude's advice advises us to make clear what the faith is when faith is distorted, whether by outside opponents or by Christians who distort the Gospel. But does this one exhortation require Christianity to become such a contentious, arrogant business?

The more the push for contending for certain knowledge about things unseen becomes central in the Church the more difficult it becomes for many people longing for "true faith" to think they can experience it.

How long can a person go through the motions of duteous devotion to Jesus without any accompanying certainties, if such certainties are required for "true faith?" The two "creeds" from the Book of Deuteronomy that I mentioned earlier seem to require remembering. That anyone can do.

The arguments supporting belief in God I learned in studying philosophy of religion were useless to me. Faith seemed for me a visceral matter, unmoved by mere logic or any evidential arguments that often seemed "procrustean." This was a word tossed about where I was studying philosophy of religion. It referred to theological adversaries. It meant they cut evidence to size or stretched it as needed to support their views. All the while my learned professors were using this very kind of reasoning, it seemed to me.

I tell you these things only to inform you of the place the Apostles' Creed played in my inward chaos. Somehow, in these desperate years when I wondered what I could believe, the Apostles' Creed remained an anchor for me. When I had no feelings of certainty, those words stuck with me, "I believe in God, the Father almighty, maker of heaven and earth, and in Jesus Christ, his only son, our Lord ..."

I am very grateful for the Apostles' Creed. I know that there are those people who object to the continuous repetition of set-forms like this because they rightly believe that anything we utter repeatedly may become "vain repetition.". There is always that risk.

There was the same risk for the ancient Israelites in repeating the *shema*. But God said, in effect, "Repeat it. Don't fret about 'vain repetition.' Just do it! Let these words stand before you in life. Because whatever might be your sincerity index as you say them, whatever the capacity to believe, here is the great act of life—to love the one Lord your God with all your heart, soul and strength." I later learned that the word for "your strength" in Hebrew is "your very much" (*m'odeka*). If my "very much" was modest, use whatever I've got.

Did the Apostles Compose this Creed?

We call our great statement of faith the "Apostles' Creed," yet I'm sure you have noticed it is not in the New Testament. The twelve apostles did not teach this *per se* though every remark in the Creed attempts to capture a teaching found in Scripture.

When we look at the first four centuries of Christianity we can see that beginning with the New Testament this statement coagulated, we might say, gradually. The seed of our Christian Creed is found in the *shema* that led our Jewish forbears to confess their faith in one God, the Creator of heaven and earth.

We Christians believe that the promised Messiah, the Son of God came. He asked His earliest followers at a couple of key junctures what they believed. They all, to begin with, would have said the *shema* each morning and evening. But Jesus had more in mind. Jesus asked Peter first, "Whom do [other] people say that I am?" Then He came to the question every follower of Jesus must answer, "Whom do YOU say that I am?"

When Peter said to Jesus, "You are the Christ, the Son of the living God," the Church was conceived. If we call Pentecost (Acts 2) the birthday of the Church, then Peter's personal confession that Jesus was the Son of the living God was the moment the Church was conceived. It began very small, like a zygote.

Several times in the New Testament Jesus evokes from people a confession like this. It went beyond the *shema* to include a view of Jesus. Nathaniel the skeptic, sitting behind a tree, comes out and sees Jesus. He is inwardly goaded to say, "Rabbi, you are the Son of God, the King of Israel" (John 1:50). All the disciples say at one point to Jesus, "You are the holy one of God" (John 6:68). Thomas blurts out, after seeing the risen Jesus, "My Lord and my God" (John 20:28). This we remember and confess too.

As Christianity slowly evolved away from the great parent system that did not accept that Jesus was the promised Messiah, statements like this pop up more and more often. In Acts 8:37, we read that the Jewish Ethiopian magistrate says, "I believe that Jesus Christ is the Son of God," after Philip explains to him the meaning of Isaiah 53— that he was reading as he rode back home in his chariot. Paul wrote to his son in the faith, Timothy, "Great is the mystery of godliness, 'God was manifested in the flesh'" (I Tim. 3:16). In other words, it all begins with admitting that God became flesh; Jesus was God made flesh.

More and more parts of the Jewish Scriptures were pointing toward Jesus. In fact, as the Jews developed an expansive way of thinking of their Bible, so did the Jews that came to believe Jesus was the Messiah. For the Jews this expansive thinking was called *midrash*— seeking out the meaning. For the Christians, this *midrash* became "Christology," that is, perceptions of Christ.

We risk thinking that we are acceptable to God only if we believe a certain way. There is more to it than this, but somehow it is part of that fragile thing we call faith. It may have been due to this that the author of the Epistle to the Hebrews wrote, "Faith is the assurance of things hoped for, the conviction of things not seen" (Hebrews 11:1).

In the early Church after the Apostles had left the scene, we can watch how our Apostles' Creed started to come together. Ignatius, Bishop of Antioch in the early second century wrote to some

Christians in another city, "Be deaf, therefore, when any would speak to you apart from Jesus Christ, the Son of God, who was descended from the family of David, born of Mary, who truly was born... truly suffered persecution under Pontius Pilate, was truly crucified and died, who was also truly raised from the dead. . . "was received up to the Father and sits on his right hand."

Others of the early Church teachers made similar concise statements of the Christian faith. Tertullian, a third century teacher from North Africa called this "the rule of faith." The words of the early teachers have been brought together in the second volume of Philip Schaff's wonderful work, *Creeds of Christendom*. I'll spare you this. Let me simply say that probably the Apostles' Creed, early known as the "Roman Symbol," evolved, and dates from about the seventh century as we now have it. The on-going pertinence of this statement of faith continues.

Much more important to us IS to realize that saying "I believe in God" does not mean having "psychological" certainty that what is in the Creed is true. How notoriously fickle are our psychological certainties, and how glib we can often be in what we say!

The Apostles' Creed became a personal statement for those admitted to Christian Baptism. Christian parents who drew their little ones into a covenantal relationship with God would affirm their faith in the words of the Apostles' Creed.

There is comfort in this common faith.

More is given to us in the gift of faith than this inward knowledge. What is this more? This more is demonstrated in the very first place in the Bible where the word "believe" is found. In Genesis 15:6, we are informed that "Abraham believed the Lord and it was reckoned to him as righteousness." From that point on Genesis tells us what Abraham did, not what he thought or felt. His belief looked like his wandering life as he obeyed God's command to "go to a place that I will show you." Abraham went—because he believed it was God that said "Go!". Where he went his children also went, drawn into his covenant with God as surely as they were drawn to new places their father took them.

It seems that Abraham had an advantage we don't have. He saw with his eyes the One that spoke to him. But then Abraham too had to trust what he had seen, not succumbing to the numbing feeling that must have come as nothing seemed to be happening in keeping with what this One promised. Twenty-five years, the Bible tells us, yawned between the promise for a son and the pregnancy of his aging wife, Sarah. That's a long time.

Had Abraham thought or felt that it was God who said "GO!" but never left to go, do you think the Book of Genesis would have made some comment on the psychological event in his mind —that he believed God had said "GO!"??

Belief is described in more than one way in the Bible. One of these has to do with being "born from above." This is something that happens to someone.

John tells us Jesus taught that this belief is like the look of the ancient Israelites at the bronze serpent that was set on a pole after they had been bitten by a poisonous snake in the wilderness. "Only a dying glance at the bronze serpent and you will be healed." Belief is like this glance at the serpent.

But belief and doing something seem to be inseparable; they intersect like the warp and woof of woven material.

It is not the inward thought that concedes that something is true, but the orientation of life that is the result. Indeed, the orientation of life may be the pedagogue needed by children as they learn their place in the covenant of their parents with God.

I have the sense that it is important to live aware of the tension inherent in thinking of faith as Jesus spoke of it: faith is assent and faith is obedience. If you and I find it hard to discover that inward certainty we would like to feel, we can find reassurance in remembering what the Scriptures tell us. Regardless of what we feel, let us simply follow on, as Abraham did, despite the stumbling that comes along the way.

Let us pray: "O God, we call you our Lord. We want to believe in You and in Your Son. O tame our hearts to Your obedience so that the belief which You have asked for from us may be indeed the belief that prompts obedience to You. We pray in Jesus' name, Amen.

God, the Father Almighty
I Chronicles 28:1-6 Matthew 6:1-15

One of the most comforting beliefs in life to me is that God wants to be known to us, not simply as our Creator, or as our Judge, and not merely in His Otherness as a Holy Being, but in a personal way as our Father. Thus, the Apostles' Creed reminds us that the God whom we believe, or believe in, is "the Father almighty."

In the Heidelberg Catechism that we remember so often here at Faith Church, we are reminded that God cares for us because He is not only almighty God but also a faithful Father. (Question 26).

From looking at nature we are led to think of God as almighty. God is the power behind the mind-boggling might of wind and seas, of earthquakes, volcanoes, tidal waves, tornadoes, lightning and thunder.

A child nurtured in the Old Testament knows well that God is powerful. Israel's God rescued His people from the Egyptians by opening the sea for them to cross on a dry river bed, and then closed that channel so that the Egyptian forces that followed them drowned on a now flooded path. That's power!

My wife and I read the great stories to our children as we put them to bed at night. From **Aesop's Fables** they learned practical wisdom. For example, by means of a lion and a mouse they learned that a kind act is never wasted, from an owl and a grasshopper, that flattery may get you nowhere, from a mouse and a lion that even a little one can help a grown up. Good lessons, for sure. One of our second century Church fathers, Justin, taught that the early Greeks anticipated much that is found in the Christian Gospel.

Then, to deepen their learning of our classical heritage, we read to them Homer's **Iliad** and **Odyssey**, that include accounts of curious gods that mingled with people and are often immoral and bad tempered. If nothing else, these stories put them to sleep. We explained to our children that those were different days in which people didn't know about the Bible.

Then, one evening before praying with them we begin reading Virgil's **Aeneid.** In just a few minutes they learned of a man (Aeneas) "much tossed about on land and ocean . . . to sate relentless Juno's ever-rankling ire." Part of reading these stories was telling them what some of these old turns of phrase meant. They learned that the gods of the Greeks were as spiteful as people can be. Their power was often used to hurt those that annoyed them. And our thoughtful little one asked, since Juno was a lady-god, "Daddy, why was Juno like that? Is God like that too?"

Though Israel's God indeed could be a God of wrath, capable of sending a great flood to destroy a world gone awry, and even of pondering the destruction of Israel after the golden calf episode (Exodus 32), He was not petulant.

Israel's God created all things, unlike the Mesopotamian or Greek's gods that created nothing but were themselves created. God created humanity, it seems, with a built-in sense of right and wrong. Our inclination to judge others for their misdeeds derives from this aspect of the image of God in us. The problem is that we are apt to be clear-eyed in noticing the fault in others, but less so in recognizing our own faults. God did not afflict humanity out of smallness of mind. Mercy was always in God's other hand as he punished His people for their sins. Fully knowing our faults God taught His people to think of Him personally as Father. As the psalmist put it in a verse I remember often, "He knows our frame; he remembers that we are dust" (Psalm 103: 14) But a loving father also does not ignore a child's misbehavior.

God's fatherly relationship with us includes expectations of us. If He is our Father, He expects a family resemblance in His children. We are not merely dust, but dust into which God breathed His breath.

Israel's God was not a God easily offended. He was "slow to chide and quick to bless" as we sing in Francis Lyle's beloved hymn. Thus, when we say in the Creed, "I believe in God, the Father almighty," while recognizing our failures, we are to feel reverence but not fright. We feel gratitude; fearing God is not hopeless dread. We read in the

Book of Proverbs, "The fear of the Lord is the beginning of wisdom."

When the children of Israel were being groomed for their special role in God's saving purposes for the world, God told Moses to tell the King of Egypt, "Israel is my son, my firstborn." As God's firstborn son, this suggests there would be others, a number in which we claim a place. Perhaps God's people needed to remember more often His view of them, "I am your Father."

When we read the New Testament, we are struck with how Jesus prayed to God as His Father in a unique way. He addressed God as "Abba." It is an Aramaic word, the colloquial Hebrew spoken by ordinary people. "Abba" is a word not quite like our word "Daddy," but similar. Our daughter once gave me a coffee mug inscribed with the words in Aramaic, "cool dad." The word dad was "Abba." It's comforting when one's daughter becomes a teenager and thinks you are still "cool."

Jesus kept saying "My Father," when He spoke to His disciples. In doing so He seemed to pass beyond the relationship that His fellow Jews claimed with God. They would say "our Father," but Jesus said, "My Father." He said to His antagonists, "If God were your Father, you would love me; for I proceeded forth and come from God" (John 8:42). He said, "I came forth from the Father, and am come into the world: again, I leave the world, and go to the Father." This went beyond anything his fellow Jews could say of God.

Jesus taught us that this uniqueness is a blessing that has rubbed off on us.

Before His ascension He taught His followers, a category of people that includes all who follow Him, even today, "I ascend unto my Father, and your Father; and to my God, and your God" (John 20:17).

But in recent times there has been a movement afoot that bridles at the thought of calling God "Father." The gender-struggle on earth has been imposed on heaven as well.

Concern for equality between men and women now has prompted some thoughtful folk to look back into history and suggest that calling God "Father," was only a product of those long years of patriarch-dominated civilization. It is undeniable that Israel was a patriarchal society. This may have been a factor in how they conceived of God. But the reason was good why God came to be thought of as Father, rather than Mother, or as some androgynous Father/Mother deity.

When Genesis 1: 27 tells of the creation of "Adam" in the image and likeness of God, we read, "male and female He created them." This seems to mean that to produce the image and likeness of God in this last created being, both male and female were included. This is a mystery that I would not presume to understand. But it suggests that our humanity has the two poles of male and female, both needed to reflect the image of a God that is neither male nor female. But there is more to it than this.

The argument for referring to God as Father goes along this line: since all our thinking about God is based on analogy, moving from the things we see to the God we cannot see, we assume that God was called "Father" because the word for God in Hebrew, the language of the Old Testament, is a masculine gender word, but inexplicably in plural form that actually means "Gods.".

Using a plural word for God may have been a way that ancient Israel kept from thinking of God as a male Deity. Perhaps Israel was forbidden to make a statue of God to keep from making a dual gender-specific likeness of God. Just imagine what this would have looked like!

Sometimes references to God include female imagery. The prophet Isaiah wrote about God, "Now I will cry out like a woman in travail: I will gasp and pant" (42: 14 "). And again, in a passage that Jesus may have read aloud in His home synagogue in Nazareth, the prophet writes for God, "As one whom his mother comforts, so I will comfort you" (61: 13). Jesus once wept over Jerusalem and said, "How often I would have gathered your children together as a hen gathers her brood under her wings, and you would not" (Matthew

23: 37). Indeed, the tenderness natural to a mother reflects the image and likeness of God.

We are misled if we dabble in gender equality with reference to God because of the gender inequalities that we long to redress in our societies.

It is good that our moral conscience is moving steadily in the direction of fairness and equality between women and men. But it is not a corollary to this that we should use inclusive language with reference to God. I believe that most if not all that refer to God as "He" would acknowledge that this is not because God is male. Instead, the "classical" way of referring to God did not come up with a gender-neutral term for God that was appropriate. God is a Person we believe, rather than an impersonal "it." For lack of a perfect pronoun with reference to God, we do the best we can.

Some years ago, when I was a beginning student at Princeton Seminary, my wife Bonnie attended chapel with me. She had heard me tell of the great blessing I received from President McCord's Monday messages on the Book of Revelation. The day she came to chapel with me the student who led the service got up to pray and intoned, "God, our mother." Princeton Seminary has a largeness to it that allows students to spread their wings.

Many ways to avoid calling God "Father" are now commonly employed. An Inclusive Language Lectionary calls God, "Father (and Mother)." Instead of calling God "Lord,"— "Sovereign" is proposed because "sovereign" can refer to a queen as well as to a king. Rather than calling Jesus "Son of Man," He is called "Human one." "Son of God" has been changed to "Child of God."

Some have passed beyond inclusive language to specifically female language in referring to God. One of our more progressive denominations, that I shall not identify by name, includes in its Book of Worship a prayer that reads: "You have brought us forth from the womb of your being." One theologian wrote, "This is what the Goddess symbolizes—the divine within women and all that is female in the universe ... The responsibility you accept is that you are divine, and that you have power."

Perhaps you can see how focusing on gender and equality between men and women has developed into a red-herring, a goose chase after a wish to foster more comfortable feelings about God.

So far as I know, the ancient peoples who worshipped goddesses never did so for reasons derived from a power struggle between men and women. Many of the ancient religions had gods and goddesses. Usually the idea of goddesses was derived from the fruitfulness of the earth, and the parallel fruitfulness of the womb of women. People were born from women, so they projected a female deity from whom everything came.

The goddesses sometimes had male priests. Sometimes, the societies that worshipped goddesses were very oppressive. In the old Gilgamesh Epic, the hero, Gilgamesh won't cavort with the goddess Astarte because he knows how she disposes of humans after she has lured them by her lavish allure.

I realize that most of us are slow to accept new ways of thinking, and it might be argued that all we need is a little time to get used to inclusive ways of thinking about to God.

But there is something very basically wrong in changing thinking about God merely to advance an equitable relationship between men and women. While it is true as Bishop Butler taught us back in the eighteenth century that all we know about God we know by analogy, it can take us only so far. Butler also taught that what we can "know" of things Divine can only attain degrees of probability, never absolute certainty. There was a time, I have read, when every candidate for the pastoral ministry was required to read Joseph Butler's **The Analogy of Religion**. He helped pastors maintain a sense of proportion as they spoke of matters pertaining to God.

Archeologists of the Near East have found statuettes of what they suggest might be consorts of Israel's God, and there may have been Israelites who thought of God as a male deity with a female consort. Thus, they made such little statues. But that such images of consorts of Israel's God may have been imagined by some Israelites was an aberration.

Israel had a strong penchant for borrowing ideas from its neighbor countries. Thus they demanded a king, and thus they dabbled in worshipping the deities of neighboring countries, and thus there were Israelites who tried to reshape their idea of their god.

Thinking of this compels me to suggest a few ideas about how this Father almighty speaks to us in the Bible.

I remind you that the things we think about God are not only deduced from what we experience but are taught to us specifically by revelation. The Bible came to us mysteriously through the moving of the Holy Spirit. People wrote the words of the Bible, but the words were somehow "inspired" by God. How this inspiration happened is beyond us to define.

I read recently of the Stanford physicist, Richard Taylor, who shared the 1990 Nobel Prize for his discovery of quarks. The information about atomic particles from which he got this insight had developed over time, but others hadn't recognized what he did, an insight that became a building block in modern physics.

There may be a parallel to this in the way the Bible's writers wrote of God. The words, and ideas found in the Bible are drawn from human vocabulary, from human experience. But here we trust that the words and ideas are reshaped by God in the event referred to in II Timothy 3: 16 as "God-breathed." This is what we call "Divine inspiration." Using human vocabulary and human ideas, God breathed into those words and ideas thoughts greater than human beings could achieve on their own. I sense a parallel to this in how the creation of humans is told in Genesis 2. God shaped dust into an image into which He breathed the breath of life.

What we know of God is due to His gracious communication to us, and not from the thoughtful speculations on the meaning of life by ancient peoples. God, in the Bible, has taught us to call Him "our Father." This is one of those thoughts beyond us. Why, I don't know. All I know is that this is how God chose to reveal Himself to us.

The word "Father," when referring to God, Is not a gender word. It does not teach us to think of God as male. God is neither male nor female. And to call God "Father" does nothing at all to advance the role of men over women.

Indeed, Jesus showed us that in the Kingdom of Heaven where God Is Father, all our traditional roles are reversed. God is "head of his house,". in a way different from the way many of us fathers preside over our homes. He served. When Jesus washed His disciples' feet, they saw the Son of this Almighty Father, demonstrating the ways of God's family. As our Father, God does more for us than any combination of the best efforts of earthly fathers and mothers. There is no rightful competition for one-up-man-ship in the family where the Heavenly Father presides, because He exceeds the most tender care we parents can offer our children.

A problem that probably affects how we think of God as Father derives from failures of many of us fathers. We do well to strive to mimic the care of our heavenly Father, so that it may be easier to think of God rightly.

Let us pray: Lord God, our Father Almighty, we bless you for your immense love for us. We thank you for your patience with our bungling race that is so often confused and troubled. Grant us the joy of remembering that you are our Father, able to provide for and be to us all that we need . Help us to honor you as is Your due. For Jesus' sake. Amen.

God, Creator of Heaven and Earth
Genesis 1:1-13; Acts 17:22-31

In the past few months, I have traveled a couple times to the big windy city just north of us. Each time I drive north on the Outer Drive along Lake Michigan and see the skyline, with its skyscrapers that seem to penetrate the heavens, I am in awe. I drive through the city and am fascinated with its remarkable network of streets. Some are built in weaving three-tiered over and under passes. Elevated trains transport thousands of people like ants scurrying to their work or pleasure. There is order to all this whirl. I marvel at the minds that conceived all this and at the hands that made it happen.

Each piece of glass on the exterior of those glass-framed skyscrapers was put in place by the careful efforts of some workman. Those that put the glass in place are perched precariously on scaffolds high above the ground. They affix exterior glass to sturdy grids of steel designed, perhaps as her life's work, by an architect in a distant office. I say "her" because women as well as men provided the intellectual artistry that designed all this. The ones that do the actual building of these strikingly beautiful buildings are people just like I am. Every inch of concrete road was first planned by a civil engineer, perhaps educated here at Purdue, and then was poured and smoothed by someone's hands, someone that was once a baby playing with toys. Chicago's skyline cannot help but evoke thoughts about God as Creator of the far greater vastness we think of as "all creation."

But there is not a city on earth that begins to match the spectacle of the wee eye of a gnat. That tiny organ in the body of a so small an insect contains technology that defies the genius of human engineering to mimic. Tenured professors in great universities study the eyes of fruit flies and write learned articles and great books about them. They try to copy the fruit-fly eye with their computers. They can't do it. If they could they would merit and earn global reputations, even if they could do so only theoretically.

A few years ago, a goat named Noori was cloned in the land of my birth, India. But the clone could not have been made from scratch.

We rightly marvel that scientists copied a goat God made. But no geneticist created a goat.

One of my friends studied the eye of the fruit-fly for his Ph.D. dissertation. He became a well-respected geneticist for his work. All of this about the life of a tiny creature that we swat away if it intrudes our space on a summer afternoon as we eat a peach.

I think of William Blake's little poem "The Fly:"

Little Fly
Thy summer's play
My thoughtless hand Has brushed away.
Am not I
A fly like thee?

God made the fly, and God made you and me. And God gave William Blake the gift to write poetry. It is all quite remarkable.

When you and I pray, it is to an infinite Being of whom the Psalmist writes that "the heavens are the work of His fingers" (Psalm 8: 3). "In His hands are the depths of the earth; the heights of the mountains are His also. The sea is His, for He made it: His hands formed the dry land" (Ps. 95:4).

If we choose not to pray, if we choose to ignore Him, or to deny He exists still, this Creator God looms beyond us. We try to describe this when we say God is also everywhere present in His creation. But it isn't in the same way that you or I are present in any place. There is an analogy between our presence somewhere and God's presence everywhere. And God doesn't need to be recognized to be present.

It is hard for us to hold this idea in our minds because none of us who "create" things, be it a quilt stitched together lovingly over years, or a gourmet meal, or the design of a city like Chicago, or a poem can stand being unnoticed. We reasonably become quite attached to what we have made and are pleased to be noticed. Your quilt passes on to the hands of someone else and you lose contact with it. The day will come when a distant grandchild will not know you made it. The meal is soon ended, and its exquisite morsels are digested and ignominiously disposed.

But after God created the heavens and the earth, the heavens endured, and the earth continues to bear speechless witness to its Creator.

Thus, it was that when our early Christian forbears gathered their thoughts about God into a "Creed," they thought it important to remember as basic that God, the Father Almighty, is the Creator of heaven and earth."

They put in this little phrase because people were apt to forget that God created this world. We are too busy to notice. You and I may be too preoccupied to consider the significance of the FACT that had it not been for a special act of God a very long time ago, nothing that surrounds us on this tiny planet, a mere speck in this vast solar system, would exist. Genesis 1 tells us that God created our earth out of the "formless void" that was there when God began. All that was there is referred to as *tohu vevohu* in the Hebrew language in which Genesis was written.

The Bible does not actually tell us that God created everything out of nothing, as is often said. This idea, though not in our Bible, appears in one of the books in the Old Testament as it was known to the earliest Christians. II Maccabees 7: 28 reads: (". . . Look at the heaven and the earth and see everything that is in them and recognize that God did not make them out of things that existed."). Though not in our Protestant Bibles, this idea was planted in the minds of early Christians and was passed along, so that many people believe their Bible teaches this.

I don't know that it matters that our Creed doesn't teach us *creatio ex nihilo*, the Latin term for "creation out of nothing." It was an early philosophical issue among the old Greeks, but no one can prove either idea.

One way of translating the first verse in Genesis suggests there may have been something before that was turned into something "formless and void," *tohu vevohu* in Hebrew. But then God reshaped this into what we see as "the heavens and the earth," etc.

Some of the earliest creeds add other details, for example that God was the creator not only of the heaven and the earth, but also of, "the seas, and all that in them is," or as we have it in the Nicene Creed, "and of all things visible and invisible." There is not a thing that we can see or that we cannot see, which God's "hand" did not form.

I know that probably all of us are here this morning because we believe that God created all of this, but we may forget that God owns it too.

I have the hunch that most of us have imbibed the popular notion that we have some ownership over at least part of God's creation. Even though we have the witness of thousands of years of human history, that no one can take his property with him (or her) when they are buried. As it has been facetiously said, hearses don't pull wagons. We cling to the fiction that we own a part of what God has created. God gave our first parents dominion—they and we are superintendents—but they didn't own anything on planet earth. It is a healthful modesty to remember this.

The reason why "No trespassing" signs are put up on peoples' yards; the reason why we have national boundaries, and walls and gates that separate great homes of the wealthy from the public; the reason why we have banks with their computers full of ledgers that reckon the great balances on some of our accounts, is to preserve the fiction that people own bits and pieces of what God has made. There is a popular fiction that Bill Gates owns a lot more than the rest of us. But how does he own what he doesn't have the ability to keep? If Mr. Gates dies next week, how much would you say he owns? Obituaries may report that he was a multi-billionaire. But lying in the grave what does he own? Will he take any more dollars with him than the homeless person living on the streets of Lafayette?

Jim Elliott, one of the missionaries to Ecuador who was slain by fearful Auca Indians in 1956 wrote, "he is no fool who gives what he cannot keep to gain that which he cannot lose."

Ought not our myth about ownership to be influenced by the reality of what we can keep?

In church we try to keep some correct perspective on this as we may sing, after we take the offering, "We give thee but thine own, whate'er the gift might be: all that we have is Thine alone, a trust, O Lord, from Thee."

But practically speaking do we not function as though this song expresses the myth, and we live the reality?

To say, "I believe in God, the Father almighty, Creator of heaven and earth," presents a reality check that we need particularly in a day in which we are fascinated with illusions, in particular, the appeal of wealth.

Part of my surprise, indeed shock, at the success of the film and video industry and its considerable interest for many intelligent people, is that everyone knows that what is seen on the movie or TV screen is entirely make believe. "Jurassic Park" may approximate animals that once existed, but we know the movie is altogether fiction. Stephen Spielberg's masterpieces of cinema technology display what people refer to as his "creative genius." But there is absolutely nothing which Spielberg created. His celluloid wonders are just that.

Each reel of film, that captures his fantasies, if touched by a small flame would disappear. We say, "I believe in God, Creator of heaven and earth." in order to re-educate ourselves about what is real.

But there is more. When you and I remember that God created the heavens and the earth, that is, EVERYTHING, we include ourselves. God made you and me. If we belong anywhere and to anyone, it is to the One who gave us life. I am tempted every day to forget. I'm too busy to remember I live because God gave me life.

Sometimes when I am tired, I turn on the television and watch people hawking a wide array of gadgets that promise to make people's lives better. I notice that Nordic Tracks offer much promise of a body changed from dumpy to heroic proportions. Of course, the footnote of this ad should be more emphasized than the product, that you must use the Nordic Track for it to be of benefit. I see amazing techniques for making hair grow on bald or balding scalps.

I am amazed at the claims made by the merchants of cosmetics—illusions of sight and smell, that promise to enhance us aging fellows' seeming virility.

Very often, after getting something new, I am struck by the fact that my life was not made happier because I have it. I find I like my old things and even my threadbare sport jackets, better than my new clothes—to my wife's periodic annoyance. I find I am more content when I have fewer things than when I have many things. Maybe it's because I've lived long enough to realize how impermanent are all these things. I really like Socrates' remark, I was told, as he walked through the agora in Athens. "Look at all the things I can do without."

When we say "I believe in God, Creator of heaven and earth." we are acknowledging what is basic. It was not a fatalistic whimper that compelled Job to say after learning of the death of his children, "The Lord gave, and the Lord takes away. Blessed be the name of the Lord." This One who gives and takes away can thus "sanctify to us our deepest distress," even the loss of every temporary thing.

There is one last aspect of this great affirmation of faith I have thought it useful to spell out. When we speak about God the Creator, you and I may have in mind a distant Being, the God of Genesis 1 who created by a word from afar. God, we think of mostly as far away. You and I may take too much to heart the psalmist's exclamation and question, "When I consider thy heavens, the work of thy fingers, the moon and the stars which Thou hast established, what is man that Thou art mindful of him, or the son of man that Thou visitest him?"

The second creation account tells of a Creator present crafting Adam from dust. God forms an image that looked like Him, which means like you and me too. Then He breathed into the nose of that form the "breath of life" so that it became a "living soul." This says something about our breath, which, though like the breath of every breathing creature, is in an inexplicable way unique.

The strange account of the "building" of Eve in Genesis 2 presents an anesthesiologist Deity, putting Adam to sleep, then taking a rib from his side to build from it a woman. The actual verbs describing God's work in the Hebrew of Genesis 2 are "form" for Adam and "build" for Eve. God formed Adam and built Eve. This describes the work of a present Divine craftsman.

Adam was dazzled when he awoke and saw woman, as was fitting with amazement. He called her "woman," but it's more dramatic in Hebrew, *Ishah*. This, according to a folk etymology, meant "to a man," since the Hebrew word for man sounds like *eesh*, and the "*ah*" afterwards might mean "to" or "for." This suggests the yearning that draws us to each other as man and woman. Genesis 1 tells us that God created Adam male and female, while Genesis 2 intimates that she was implicit in him from the start. She was built from Adam's side, so they would be side by side, and neither one over the other. It is possible to feel very poetic pondering these ideas.

This account of the intimacy of God in His creation is purposeful. We are reminded of it further in what transpires with the first people. God is close enough and personal enough to walk with our first parents in the beautiful garden of Eden. God was present to notice that Abel was missing so that He asked Cain, "Where is your brother?" Much later we read in Exodus 24, that Moses, Aaron, his two sons and seventy elders of Israel saw God on a mountain top. These are biblical pictures to teach us that God is not far from us, though now unseen.

I think that for very many folks their faith is in a God Who seems remote. This is strangely unsatisfying. We know that "we see through a glass darkly," as the Apostle Paul put it. But if we think about it, we see some things that are clues to the existence of more. There is uncanny intimacy in both the relationship between God and people, and in the relationship between us as man and woman.

When we pray we are using a reflex that trusts that however distant God may seem, He is near enough to hear our prayer. There is a restlessness that points to something. Inside of everyone there is a deep other "ingredient;" we call that perceptor the "heart."

In the Old Testament it is sometimes referred to as the kidneys, as in Psalm 26 2 where the psalmist writes, "Prove me, O Lord . . . test my kidneys and my heart." (Though this unfamiliar term—pronounced *kilyote* in Hebrew is often changed in modern translations to "heart.") Pascal called it a "God-shaped vacuum." St. Augustine described it in his *Confessions* the restlessness of the human heart."

Whatever it is called, there is something deep in us that resonates with the words of the Apostle Paul, "all things were created through Him and for Him. He is before all things, and in Him all things hold together" (Col. 1:15-17).

I learned recently from a new history of the Hasidim, the strain of Judaism that awakened in 18th century Poland, of Rabbi Ya'akov Yosef, a friend of the Baal Shem Tov, the movement's founder, who wrote, "If thoughts arise while one is studying Torah or praying they are but a garment or covering in which God is hiding."

Here he brought home what the Psalmist asked, "Where can I flee from your presence? Even if I make my bed in *sheol*, you are there" Psalm 139: 7-8). *Sheol* is the place of the dead, which another psalm laments that it is a place of silence (Psalm 115: 17). Where God seems absent he is just hiding, as Isaiah put it, in what seems like an expression of awe rather than a complaint (Isaiah 45: 15).

It is impossible to think of God's nearness in this way without slipping into thoughts of the next statement of the Creed. The wonderful, surprising mystery of the Gospel is that the Creator came in a thirty-year period when he was both seen and heard.

The heart of the Gospel is that God took on human flesh. "He became perfectly man," as a fourth-century statement of faith put it (Creed of Epiphanius). This may parallel metaphor of God's presence in Genesis 2, when He formed the first human from the dust and built woman from one of this human's ribs. God was present beside humans then, but in Christ, God became human.

Paul told the Athenian eggheads that their philosopher, Epimenides, was correct when he said of this God, "In Him we live and move and have our being." But they didn't understand how this was so.

The Gospel in effect tells us not only that we have our being in God, but that He became for a time human.

I know that I am delving into the ineffable, which means what is indescribable in human language. But it is not wrong to try, particularly if one's motivation is gratitude. Trying to understand is an expression of gratitude.

This is very hard to figure out, but like many things we place our trust in for much less significant aspects of life, we don't have to be able to figure it out but only to trust that it is so.

Here again I realize I am leaping ahead to what we will read further on in the Creed. I wonder if it is helpful to get some gist of the Incarnation if we recognize the miracle of ordinary human conception. In conception from a tiny wriggling seed and an egg something is formed with unspeakable complexity. It begins in an act of love mingling the bodies of a man and a woman. In their ecstasy all the ingredients of their heredity ignite what might become a Mozart or an Einstein or a Madame Curie, or tragically even a Hitler. What will become of that beginning human is as unknown as what will become of human history.

God has planted intimacy in our hearts. It is a great tragedy when the parallel intimacy we are offered as human beings along with our intimacy with our Creator is obscured by desecrations of the intimacy most immediately known to us. The God who formed us with His hands, breathed into man's nose His breath, and then built woman from breathing Adam's side, intends that an exquisite love will bind us to each other and to Him. This tells us something also of the sacredness of our bonding in human marriage. It reflects the intimacy of our Creator with us.

This far outdoes the mystery of electricity, or how the moon affects the tides, or how a sunny day spawns optimism while a rainy Monday "gets me down." We live as if all these "miraculous" aspects of the miracle of this world are quite ordinary—as they are. Indeed, how miraculous is the ordinary! The things of God take place alongside the ordinary, that is itself miraculous, though so often seen that it is called "the ordinary."

A favorite hymn of mine asks God to "Open my eyes that I may see glimpses of truth Thou hast for me." When we say the Creed in phrases, it is hard to keep from realizing that "glimpses" God the Father almighty offers us through this medium, includes what we specifically will say we believe in phrases just ahead. So now I must conclude lest I move even farther ahead.

Let us pray: "Lord God, Creator of heaven and earth, and of all things seen and unseen, grant to us some understanding of these matters about which we speak. In Jesus' name, Amen.

I Believe in Jesus Christ, God's only Son
Genesis 14:17-20; John 3:16-21

Let us look now at the second part of the Apostles' Creed. Its structure has four parts: the first three are about the triune God, Father, Son, and Holy Spirit. The fourth part has to do with the Church. The point of this is that people are important to God. The people-part is "the Church." Now we begin to ponder the second part.

I would guess nearly all of us that are interested enough in the Apostles' Creed to be reading this book have repeated these words many times. "I believe in Jesus Christ, His only Son." But whether you, my dear reader, know the Creed, every Christian, by definition, believes not only in God the Father, but also in God the Son, Jesus Christ.

There is no danger today in confessing this. You will not stand out in the crowd as you say the Creed here on the Lord's Day. Your voice will blend with the sound of many others.

In the early days when this brief statement of faith was being forged, confessing belief in Jesus Christ as God's Son took some courage.

One day, early in the second century, a man by the name of Ptolemaeus was accused before a judge of being a Christian. He was accused by the disgruntled husband of a woman to whom he had spoken about Jesus. When Ptolemaeus was brought before Urbicus, the judge, he was asked one question: "Are you a Christian?" When he answered, "Yes" he was led off at once to be executed. A man in the crowd, named Lucius, saw what had happened. He stood up to protest this sentence. "Why did you pass such a sentence?" he asked. "Was this man convicted of a crime? Is he an adulterer, a murderer, or a thief?" The judge answered him. "It seems that you are a Christian too!" Lucius replied, "I am." He was promptly executed too. A third Christian stood up and protested this, and he was immediately executed.

In these early years of people dangerously following the Way of Jesus, Justin Martyr, wrote an eloquent appeal to the Emperor

Antoninus Pius, who was a philosopher. He told the emperor that he should not impose the death penalty on Christians simply because of the name "Christian."

One of his interesting arguments that may have made the emperor smile, was the similarity of the Greek word for "anointed one," or Christ, "*Christos*" to the Greek word for "excellent," *chrestos*. Of course, the *Christos* was *chrestos*, indeed, ineffably so.

When we read Justin's "Apology" against this background we realize that much has changed. We confess this faith without danger, at least without danger of persecution.

Not realizing how significant this confession of faith in Christ was to a Christian, some of the Roman governors compassionately tried to make it possible for them to actually avoid violating their beliefs by just pretending to offer a token gesture of "worship" to the emperor. Just do the act. Say nothing.

Polycarp's reluctant executioners told the aging bishop of Smyrna, on February 23rd, A.D. 155 to do this. This was in the days of the same emperor of Rome to whom Justin Martyr wrote his" Apology." Polycarp refused any gesture of denying Jesus by even a hint at worshipping the emperor. He said something I have not been able to forget, ever since I read it many years ago: "Eighty and six years have I served Him, and He has done me no wrong. How can I blaspheme my King who saved me?" He was then burned at the stake.

How different is our day when our land is sometimes referred to as a "Christian nation!" If you let it be known at work that you believe in Jesus Christ, you may be labeled a fanatic or a kook, labels nobody enjoys, but you'll not be executed. In fact, it may become a social asset. You may become part of a popular majority.

What do we mean when we call Jesus Christ "God's Son?"

The Gospels of Matthew (1: 18-24) and Luke (1: 31-35) begin by letting us know that Jesus of Nazareth was conceived in a way no other person's life began. Each of us has a mother and a father. Jesus too, but not as we do. In fact, these two Gospels tell us He had no earthly father. Joseph was referred to as Jesus' father, because he was His father legally.

You have often heard of the Virgin Birth of Jesus, but we should rather refer to His mother's "virgin conception." His birth was like anyone's birth. How Jesus' mother became pregnant was unique. Neither the Gospel of Mark nor the Gospel of John report Jesus' virginal conception. Nor does the Apostle Paul refer to it explicitly.

In fact, Paul seems to respond to the reported apparent scandal of Jesus' paternity in II Corinthians 5: 21 when he writes, "For our sake he [i.e., God] made Him (Jesus) to be sin who knew no sin." One Jewish reference to Jesus was as a *mamzer*, which means bastard. It is a Hebrew word found in Deuteronomy 23: 2 with the mandate that "no *mamzer* shall enter the assembly of the Lord." We know that no child is responsible for how it is conceived, but in the culture of His time a child born out of wedlock suffered from a cruel bias. The word "bastard" had more sting to it then than now when it is usually a mere expletive.

There was great risk of misunderstanding in this teaching that Jesus' only Father was His Heavenly Father. This may have been the reason for Jesus first deed as He began His life's work.

He went to the Jordan to be baptized by His cousin, John. The others in the queue with Him, waiting to be baptized, came to have their sins ceremonially washed away. They may have wondered what Jesus' offense was. Why did Jesus respond to John the Baptist's question about why he should baptize Jesus, "Thus it is fitting to fulfill all righteousness" (Matthew 3: 15)? Was it possibly because this slur on his paternity had some currency? Perhaps those in line with Him thought it was suitable for Him to receive John's cleansing baptism because He was a *mamzer*, a bastard. It seems blasphemous to think this, but Jesus suffered from being the butt of many derogatory remarks. He forfeited His merited honor when He "emptied Himself," as Paul put it in his Christ-hymn in Philippians 2.After, not before, He was immersed in the Jordan River, a voice was heard from the skies saying, "This is my beloved Son, with whom I am well pleased." At the transfiguration, later, when Peter,

James and John saw Jesus appear with Moses and Elijah, they heard a similar voice saying, "This is my beloved Son." Then this voice told them, "Listen to Him."

But it wasn't so until after Jesus' baptism. Until then He waited in a queue along with people who in merely standing there admitted to their need of this ceremonial cleansing. Had there been any inkling of Jesus identity as Son of God, people would have asked Him, "what are you doing here" But only John asked this.

It is impossible to put ourselves into the minds of those that first heard Jesus referred to as "Son of God." Israel was referred to as "My first-born son" in Exodus 4: 22. Jesus' fellow Jews knew about the distinct sacred paternity of their ancient forebears. At the burning-bush episode when Moses heard God speaking to him, God identified Himself as "the Lord, the father of Abraham, Isaac, and Jacob," and by extension of all their children. So, all were "sons" of God as descendants of Abraham.

But clearly in the New Testament, more is meant than this group sonship of God. One of the classes I teach at Purdue introduces us to the stories discovered etched in clay tablets in ancient Mesopotamia. One of these is about a king of Uruk named Gilgamesh. He was two-thirds deity and one-third man. Much later, some of the Roman emperors identified themselves as gods. But the Jews had no such idea to play with in their minds with regard to Jesus.

Jesus was the Son of the heavenly Father in a way nobody else could be. We modern people who are blessed with all the information of modern biology and genetics, are asked to believe this just as someone who lived in the days when most people thought the earth was flat.

To refer to Jesus as "the Christ," did not automatically imply "Son of God." The Christ means "the Messiah," an Anglicized form of its Hebrew equivalent, *meshiach*. For the Jews this one anointed to deliver them from their oppressors would be fully human, not in the least Deity. He would be a descendant of King David, with military muscle; just that. The proof of this would be, as we say, "in the eating," that is, in his success in routing their enemies and bringing Israel back to live in peace in Jerusalem and then bringing peace to the world.

But the Christian understanding of the Messiah's role was a deliverance from an enemy far different from the enemy that was Rome. The real enemies were what wrecked humanity inwardly, that crushed the human spirit, sin, and death. These were the enemies the Messiah was to conquer. Nothing like this happened when Jesus walked the dusty roads of Israel.

There is a parallel between the Genesis 1 creation account in which "the spirit (or wind) of God hovered over the surface of the waters and God's promise through Jeremiah (31: 33) that He would write on the hearts of the Jews, His people, a new covenant. It would replace the covenant written on tablets of stone, given to Moses (Exodus 34: 1). At first the laws were chiseled into that stone, but Jeremiah said God would write on their hearts.

In Jewish tradition the Feast of Pentecost came to be thought of as the Festival marking God's giving to Israel the Torah, the Law. At the first Christian Pentecost described in Acts 2, at this feast of the giving of the Law a powerful wind of God blew through an upstairs room in Jerusalem. A new breath of God blew into the nostrils of the small body of those that gathered in the Upper Room in Jerusalem. What Jeremiah wrote about the law being written in the hearts of God's people is parallel to this new animation, this new wind from God that animated a small cluster of fearful people so that they became a witnessing community. This wind was like the wind at the beginning of creation separating the waters of the abyss. Putting text beside text I see the connection between Jeremiah's promise of a new covenant and the new work of creation suggested at the first Christian Pentecost. Now God's law was written on their hearts.

The parallels to the creation account in Genesis 1 and this moment are tantalizing to ponder. At the beginning there was just "formless and void," an abyss, before God began to create. God began to create by having this "wind of God" (*ruah Elohim*) hover over the surface of the waters. The Hebrew word for "wind" is equally well translated "spirit." Thus, many Christians interpret the Genesis 1 "wind" as "the Holy Spirit," that is, the third person of the Holy Trinity.

This is jumping the gun, however. I don't see the Trinity is hinted at in Genesis 1. This is imposed on the Creation story by Christians who look for intimations of the Trinity in the Old Testament.

But beyond question, the need of the human heart is reflected in the "formless and void" of the state of this planet before the work of creation began. Jeremiah used the same words describing the "formless and void" that was Israel in their disarray as they went into exile (4: 23). Of Israel he wrote, "For my people are foolish, they know me not; they are stupid children, they have no understanding. They are skilled in doing evil, but how to do good they know not." Then comes his reference to this planet prior to creation: "I looked on the earth and lo it was formless and void, and to the heavens and they had no light." The verses that follow describe a state as abject as the earth before God began to create it from the formless void.

When the Apostle Paul referred to the one "in Christ" as a "new creation" (II Corinthians 5: 17), he pointed back to Jeremiah's forecast of a new covenant. There was a momentum drawn from the Old Testament that prompted the Christian inference that Jesus was not only the Christ," that is, the Anointed One, who would conquer humanity's bitter foes, but also "the Son of God."

Though John's Gospel doesn't refer to the "virgin birth" of Jesus, it identifies Him in a way that is congruent with Jesus' unique conception. "He was in the beginning with God and was God. All things were made by Him . . . "

In the next section I will discuss the virgin birth as clearly as I can. The New Testament writers interpreted Old Testament texts in light of their new understanding of what God did in Jesus' miraculous birth.

Another passage in Isaiah also must be read differently than it ordinarily was understood. For example in Isaiah 9: 6 we read of the "child born to us," "the son given to us," that his names would include, "wonderful counselor, mighty God, everlasting father, prince of peace," which to Christians seem fully appropriate to apply to Jesus. His triumphant function is described in Isaiah 9: 7, "Of the increase of his government and of peace there will be no end on the throne of David . . . to establish it . . . with justice and righteousness from this time forth and for evermore." This did not seem to any of Jesus' fellow Jews to refer to Him in any way at all. The Jewish expectation was of an anointed one like David, a Jewish king born in the way all humans are born in David's lineage. He would bring peace and stability to the Jews, overthrowing the Roman government of their day. Clearly, Jesus didn't accomplish this.

Something the early Christians learned from their fellow Jews, that we fail to recognize, is that we not only read the Bible, but we also think about what we read—and thinking about it is part and parcel of reading it. What "the Bible says" is what we think it means. What we think it means is what we think God says. Much of what we say, when we say, "the Bible says," or what "God says," is what we think the Bible means. That this is so nobody can fairly deny. And it is not an accusation to make this charge.

The Jews have a concept of "oral Torah," that referred to God's on-going communication to His people. God not only gave them the "written Torah," but He also instigated the on-going insights from it. In fact, they believe that this "Oral Torah" was implicit in what Moses received from God on Mt. Sinai.

Something like this happened, I believe, in the Greek translation's rendering of the Hebrew words in Isaiah. This new insight became pivotal to the Christian understanding of the meaning of the Bible. And this informed their acceptance of the writings now comprising the "New Testament."

As the Jews accept the Mishnah (second century AD) and the Talmud (fifth century AD) as written forms of the Oral Torah, that began when Moses received the stone tablets of the Law on Mt. Sinai, Christians accept the New Testament as the fulfillment of the Old Testament and equally "God-breathed."

We trust the New Testament's interpretation of the ancient biblical texts. As I have shown my students the range of Jewish interpretations of the Hebrew Bible, they have not always been convinced that these interpretations were on target. But we too risk adding to and taking away from Scripture when we too self-confidently interpret it to fit with themes we have developed and declared to be the meaning of the Bible. While we ask the Holy Spirit's aid in understanding the Bible, if we interpret the meaning of the Bible without modesty we err.

The tragedy of this is that we don't need to do this for the Scriptures to speak to us. In fact, the safest way to read the Bible with understanding is to acknowledge that "God's thoughts are not our thoughts," as the prophet Isaiah put it (Chapter 55). In fact, this happened within Scripture itself.

In the second Psalm, David writes something we wonder what he meant: "I will tell of the decree of the Lord: He said to me, 'You are my son, today I have begotten you.'" Was David arrogant? He remembered that Samuel had called him "the Lord's anointed." But he knew the boundaries between himself, as the Lord's anointed king, and God. We wonder what David understood as he wrote these words.

The tension between human understandings and the meaning of the sacred text has been part of the dance of faith of the ancient Jews and of their heirs in the Christian faith. The Jews understood various levels of meanings as a "grid" through which to ponder the meaning of their Scriptures. The early Christians tapped into their insights to understanding the sacred text.

The Apostle Paul in Galatians 4 employs the Jewish allegorical interpretation to understand a deeper meaning of Sarah and Hagar as mothers of Abraham's sons, Ishmael and Isaac. Again in I Corinthians 10 Paul used allegory to point out a deeper than obvious meaning of Moses hitting the rock to get water, described in Exodus 17.

The 4th-century Christians who put together the Nicene Creed described Jesus as "begotten, not made." If Jesus were "made" as you and I were, it would mean that just as you and I once did not exist, so there was a time that Jesus did not exist. Arius, considered a heretic in the fourth century, thought this of Jesus. The Gospel of John teaches us that Jesus was in the beginning with God. He always existed. But in John's Gospel we read, "He was in the beginning with God." He was begotten, that is, born of the Virgin Mary, but His existence did not begin then.

Somehow Jesus became evident as this something more to those that He gathered into his small group of friends. To call His disciples "friends" applies to this holy cluster a kind of association that gathered around rabbis in those days called "*haberim*," friends. Other clusters of "friends," I think, recognized a uniqueness in Jesus among charismatic leaders of the day. It was said of Jesus, "He teaches not as the rabbis, but with authority" (Matthew 7: 29).

At a pivotal moment in His life with the disciples, as He sat with them in a cave at Caesarea Philippi, Jesus asked Peter, "Whom do you say that I am?" And Peter replies, "You are the Christ, the Son of the living God." Jesus gets excited, as we never see Him excited at any other time. I feel His animation when He bursts out, "Blessed are you, Simon Bar-Jonah! For flesh and blood has not revealed this to you, but my Father in heaven." Then Jesus seems to have inaugurated the Church. "I tell you, you are Peter, and on this rock, I will build my church, and the powers of death shall not prevail against it." Jesus obviously was overwhelmed by this confession from Peter. It was a major break-through when Peter made the leap from recognizing that Jesus was the Christ, to understanding that He was also the Son of God.

Yet, in the Gospel of Mark we read that Jesus wants to preserve this as a secret. This is a puzzle to all that read Mark's Gospel.

At Jesus' trial, the crucial moment of His antagonists' anger comes after the High Priest presses Him with the question, "Are you the Christ, the Son of God," and Jesus replies, "You have said so." This was a somewhat cryptic way of saying, "You're quite right." Then the High Priest tore his robes, aghast and outraged at this blasphemy. Jesus did not aggressively teach this as part of His message. In the heat of His trial He did not deny it.

After Jesus rose from death, "doubting Thomas" saw Him, but rather than exclaiming the obvious—You're alive!—Thomas breaks out in worship. "My Lord and my God." It is odd that we should call Thomas, "doubting Thomas," when all the disciples doubted Jesus' resurrection. We don't call Peter, "denying Peter" because on one occasion he denied Jesus three times.

If you and I are Christians it matters that we realize something of the immensity of this confession of faith. While it may become vain repetition to say it often, nevertheless, say it.

Practically speaking it is evident to me that we American Christians need a shot in the arm that would come from the "spell" of remembering again that our "religion" is something far more profound than a cultural quirk of the Western world.

Hints of God's special presence in this world were perceived long ago by other religions but were always given strange mythical expressions. But the devoted followers of these other religions often became very intense in their reverence toward the God they perceived and whom they told of in their stories.

Hinduism's ancient wisdom perceived that Vishnu, the second person in their triad of Brahma, Vishnu, and Siva, took on strange *avatars*—appearances. But their legends depict him appearing not only as Lord Krishna, but also as a tortoise, a fish, a monkey, a man-lion and a dwarf.

When I read of these remarkable stories in other religions, I think of what Paul wrote in Romans 1:20— "Ever since the creation of the world, his invisible nature, namely, his eternal power: and deity, has been clearly perceived in the things that have been made." In his years as a missionary in India, my father often felt that the devotion of many Hindus trumped the devotion of many Christians, even missionaries, despite the oddness he saw in the specifics of their heritage.

When I look back at the beginning of the Christian Church I see that those nearest to Jesus saw Him in a way that inspired a devotion of their whole lives to Him, even at great cost of suffering or death.

They saw no mythical tortoise or fish, a God in disguise. They saw the God who created us in His own image, take on this image again, for people's sake. As Paul wrote of Jesus, "He was made in the likeness of man."

What we need today is a fresh glimpse of Jesus, the Son of God that will teach us again, as Clement wrote, to "bow the knees of our hearts before Him."

One of my good friends, Bill Placher, now of blessed memory, wrote a book he called, **The Domestication of Transcendence.** He lamented how casually we have responded to the mysterious facts at the heart of our Gospel.

I want to urge us all to so think of Jesus that we see Him not just as Mary's darling Son, a great miracle worker and teacher, who died and rose again and somehow founded the Church. He is not just the One who provided us the wonderful festivals of Christmas and Easter that are so much a part of American cultural life. Belief in Him for us now is as belief in God was in the days of Abraham. For Abraham it was not a theological point of view to believe God, but a summons to a way of life. I doubt that Abraham thought "theologically." But his faith plunged him into a devoted life of trusting God. He had never heard of Christ, yet he remains forever the model for our faithfulness, which is the "life of faith."

Let us pray: O Lord God, heavenly Father, how plainly You showed us Your heart in letting Your Beloved Son be born to a human mother. Grant us to so revere, honor, and worship the Lord Jesus, that our whole lives will be devoted to Him—in our waking and working, even in our sleeping and dreaming. In Jesus' name. Amen.

Jesus Christ, our Lord
Isaiah 44:1-8; Acts 16:25-34

When Christians say the Apostles' Creed and come to the second part, we follow up referring to Jesus Christ God's only Son" with "**our Lord**." It comes out in a flow as though one thing was being said about Jesus. But really three things are being said. We are affirming first our belief in the man, Jesus of Nazareth, second in the fact that this Man was the only Son of God, and third we are claiming Him as our Lord. It is like the phrase in the *shema, adonai echad elohenu,* "the Lord, our God, one Lord." I think we might do well to say this phrase as though it had two commas in it: "and in Jesus Christ, God's only Son, our Lord."

A significant difference between the Apostles' Creed and the Nicene Creed is that in the latter, we are making a joint public claim about Jesus Christ's relationship to us. In the Apostles Creed we begin, not "We believe, but "I believe . . ." This became a statement of faith Christians would confess at baptism.

We remember Jesus Himself taught us that there is an individual aspect to a public acknowledgement of His lordship. In Matthew 16: 13 we hear Jesus ask his disciples, "Who do people say that I am?" And then, "Who do you say that I am?" Earlier in Matthew's Gospel we read that Jesus said, "Not everyone who says to me, 'Lord, Lord,' shall enter the kingdom of heaven, but he who does the will of my Father who is in heaven. On that day many will say to me, 'Lord, Lord, did we not do many things in your name?' And then will I declare to them, 'I never knew you; depart from me, you evildoers" (Matt. 7:21-23). This shows us the particularity of our responsibility in our individual confessions of faith.

There is great value to our making public professions of faith as part of our Lord's Day worship, as we regularly do in the congregation in which I now worship. And there is great value of standing together and listening to one another profess our faith on the Lord's Day. That great sound of many people reciting the Creed is a moving sound. This is, indeed, of great value to us. But we do well to remember the tension that is part of our professions of faith.

As I tried to point out in the first part of this reflection on the Apostles' Creed, "belief" is a difficult thing to explain. Our personal limitations feed into our capacity to believe. Nevertheless, there is rightfully an expectation of "sincerity" when we say the Creed. Regardless of what or how we understand what we are saying, there is a seriousness about this moment comparable to the seriousness of those early Christians who may not have completely understood Jesus, but were in earnest when they said, "I believe in Jesus Christ, my Lord" as they stood before the Roman magistrate, who could sentence them to death.

The word "Lord" was used by the earliest Christians to refer to Jesus. It was a word that translated the name of God in the Hebrew Bible. The Jews came to have such reverence for this name that they did not pronounce it as it was spelled, something like YHWH. They pronounced it "*Adonai*," which happens to be the ordinary term for "master" or "lord," as we would use the term, "lord of the manor."

Psalm 8 begins with the words, "O Lord our Lord." In our English translations this phrase "Lord" appears both times. The first time it refers to the name of God, and the second time it refers to His "rank," as Israel's Master. The NRSV translates the second of these two, "our Sovereign." "O Lord our Sovereign." The difference is obvious when you read it in the Hebrew Bible where the two "Lords" are spelled differently.

In the Gospel of Mark, the first of the Gospels to be written, from the beginning Mark associates Jesus with the Lord referred to by the Old Testament prophet Malachi when he wrote, "Prepare the way of the Lord." He wrote this, of course, well after Jesus was no longer with the disciples. But what drew the disciples to Jesus was this uncanny sense they had about Him that they probably could not explain. But in coming to Him, regardless of what they understood about Jesus they participated in what the prophet had predicted, accepting Him in a way that was both like and different from the way other rabbis gathered followers.

It was an uncanny attraction, we'd have to say. I use the term "uncanny" to accentuate the fact that what attracted the earliest disciples to Jesus exceeded anything they could have explained. What would it take to persuade ordinary fishermen to drop everything, leaving behind wives and children to follow him? They did not know their joining His society would be a metaphor for what would become Christianity, a society much larger than the original twelve.

Similarly, beliefs we have about Jesus are beyond the capacity of ordinary vocabulary, or of explanation, or of proofs to verify. Jesus used no "evidential apologetics" to demonstrate that He was Incarnate God, a description that was later understood. What we refer to as "proofs" of His Deity, His miracles, had, I think, counterparts with other Jewish spiritual leaders, some of whom could perform miracles.

There were in those days Jewish circles gathered around teachers. The teachers were called rabbis. As Bruce Chilton has written of some of them, "these rabbis cured sickness and relieved drought through prayer: that was the mark of divine compassion working through them" (***Rabbi Jesus,*** p. 109). Jesus was often addressed as "Rabbi" because He did such works.

We believe that there was more to Jesus than what the eye can see because we have read of this "more" in the Gospels. But our conviction is more than book-learning. We are convinced inwardly. This inward convincing goes far beyond any "Demonstration of the Gospel," as Eusebius, the fourth century Church historian called one of his great works. I am aware that I may have an immense feeling of this "more" while being unable to explain what is giving me this feeling. I am often overwhelmed when I take Communion, though I cannot explain the "substitutionary atonement." If someone asked me, "why the tears," I could only reply something like, "I stand amazed in the presence of Jesus." No, I don't believe the bread and the wine become the body and blood of Jesus. But I do believe that at the Eucharist Jesus is more nearly "physically" present than in any other time. Maybe I feel annoyed that I must expose this very personal response as I take the bread and the wine.

Again, I'm reminded of the Jewish denomination called Hasidism, that began in the eighteenth century and that bears resemblances to early Christianity. Modern Hasidim in Brooklyn still cherish their former Rebbe, Rabbi Menachem Mendel Schneerson. Their attachment to him transcends the loyalty of most small societies to their leaders. Leaders come and go. But Rabbi Schneerson stays, somehow. He was their *Tsaddik*, a title that meant an unusual man, uncannily righteous who "attaches himself in *devekut* (communion or union) with God" (**Hasidism; A New History *[*Princeton UP, 2017*]*,** p. 151) He was the go-between for his followers with God. Rabbi Schneerson died many years ago (January 17, 1951), yet his followers await his return. Where did this idea come from?

The New Testament (I Timothy 2: 5) declares of Jesus, "There is one God and one mediator between God and man, the man Christ Jesus." But as mediator he was more than a go-between. The epistle to the Hebrews describes the direct access we have via a new covenant in which Christ is both mediator and sacrifice (9: 25-26).

When Jesus was called "Lord" it was in a distinct association with the One referred to as YHWH by ancient Israel. Yet we Christians do not associate fear with Jesus as Lord the way fear was a reasonable part of the way Israelites thought about God.

It is true, fear or reverence for God is the beginning of wisdom, as the Proverb says, but there is more comfort than fear in claiming Jesus Christ as our Lord. We are not just saying publicly that Jesus is to be obeyed; we are acknowledging that Jesus is Lord of all, of everything, of me. The Apostle Paul wrote of Him "He is the image of the invisible God, the first-born of all creation; for in Him all things were created, in heaven and on earth, visible and invisible . . . He is before all things and in Him all things hold together" (Colossians 1: 15-17).

Of us too we might say, as we read in Genesis 1, that we are images of the invisible God. But Paul describes Jesus' uniqueness in words that reach toward the ineffable.

All of this is more than mere theory. When earthquakes crush the life out of tens of thousands of people in India, and floods destroy not only farm land and homes along the Mississippi, and thousands of poor people and animals in Bangladesh, or when Bosnian Christian Serbs shell the life out of their Muslim neighbors, or when cancer strikes your dearest friend, or when you lose your job, this doesn't mean that chaos has taken over the world. To be sure the miseries are real, and we wish God would fix this broken world. But, no matter what, "Jesus Christ, God's only Son, our Lord holds all things together. All is not lost."

The earliest Christians who taught us what we believe, lived in a world not alien to suffering. When things were "falling apart, they (and we) were taught by the Apostle Paul, "By Him all things hold together."

Very often this may seem the most ridiculous remark one could make. But essential to our faith is accepting the mystery of this confidence in the face of the evidence.

Indeed, you might respond, "If Jesus Christ is holding things together, I'd hate to see things fall apart." It's kind of like saying, after being hurt by a friend, "Who needs enemies?"

I have a strong hunch that the moment you and I are slipping from this life into the next, we will see a clear sense of beautiful order that lets us know that all the chaos we thought we saw was merely superficial. Underneath the surface was something we might want to describe as "everlasting arms"—something strong, permanent, and very loving.

We will understand that in what we then called "life" we devoted a disproportionate amount of attention to the body, to physical and material things. We were fooled into thinking that the real things were the things we could see and feel, buy and consume, aspire to and achieve, while the tugs at our conscience and the moments of intuition of something deeper going on, were unreal— merely bits of undigested beef, as Ebenezer Scrooge described the apparitions that appeared to him on Christmas Eve.

We will then understand the reality that Paul describes in Romans 8:38— "I am sure than neither death, nor life, nor angels, nor principalities, nor things present, nor things to come, nor powers, nor height nor depth, nor anything else in all creation, was able to separate us from the love of God in Christ Jesus **our Lord**."

A good part of our difficulty in understanding Jesus Christ as Lord has to do with Jesus' difference from other authorities we have experienced. If you have never stood before a judge, perhaps you have watched a court-room drama. I have sat in a courtroom and heard a judge sentence a man named Amos King to death. I was character witness for him because he and I had exchanged letters for several years. I testified in his behalf. The prosecuting attorney asked the judge that I be asked to leave the courtroom when they gave their final argument. Afterward, this attorney approached me and told me that she thought my testimony was so persuasive that the prosecution would lose its case. I found no comfort in learning this, as I heard his death sentence announced, though I appreciated her saying it to me. The judge too was an ordinary mortal who, too, would die. So much power and authority in that black-robed middle-aged man. He spoke severely as befits someone who can sentence a person to death. But we knew nothing about his past, and what matters of his life were unknown, that might have made us think differently about his right to condemn another man to death.

The Gospels show us a Jesus whose Lordship was different from the characteristic human judge. The Gospel of Mark shows us this humble man who one day will preside at the "judgment seat of Christ." John's baptism drew to him people who felt the weight of God's judgment. Jesus identified Himself so completely with sinning people that He stood in line with them to be baptized. The people standing before and behind Him had no idea that He was any different from the rest of them—who came to repent of being unfair tax-collectors, or of being brutal soldiers, or of being hypocritical religious leaders.

The Gospel of John tells us of a rabbi named Jesus who washed His disciples' feet on the eve of His betrayal to condemning Roman procurator. Among those whose feet He washed was His betrayer's.

When He went into the synagogue of Capernaum and was invited to explain the Bible passages that had been read, it dawned on those who heard Him that He taught differently than others who taught. Mark says, "He taught them as one who had authority, and not as the scribes."

I wonder what the uniqueness was in Jesus' teaching. His tone of voice was probably gentle rather than stentorian—like a Greek herald. Maybe He spoke softly when there was just the thirteen of them, so that they had to lean forward to hear. But on a mountain side His voice projected, perhaps multiplying His voice as He multiplied five small loaves and two small fish so that they were enough to feed thousands. Those that heard Him may have caught the inkling that there was a complete conformity between the way He lived and the way the Bible said one ought to live. When we encounter holiness in life, it grabs us. Jesus' holiness caught their imagination.

Mark shows us that when Jesus encountered the demonic world, that world of dark spiritual powers most of us Westerners have been lulled into believing does not exist, the demons recognized Him and complained loudly, "What have you to do with us, Jesus of Nazareth? Have you come to destroy us?" Ordinarily, they gloated in their power to destroy people; but now in the presence of this gentle Man they were frightened.

Jesus was Lord over sickness. Before His loving touch a fever that could have killed Peter's wife's mother was helpless. In the evening many people suffering from various diseases came to Him, and His lordship over disease resulted in their being cured.

On one occasion Jesus was teaching in a crowded room and everyone heard a scraping sound on the roof. They watched debris fall and the ceiling tiles being removed. Four men lowered a paralyzed man on a stretcher before Jesus. Obviously, they wanted Jesus to heal his body. But Jesus, who saw deeper into this fellow than his physical paralysis, said to him: "My son, your sins are forgiven." The very people who were glad Jesus could heal sick people were now outraged that He suggested He had power to forgive sin too. So, Jesus reminded them that His Lordship didn't discriminate between illnesses of the heart and illnesses of the body. He healed the paralytic so completely that he carried his own stretcher out of the house, a forgiven and healthy man.

Jesus showed His Lordship over the weather, calming a frightful storm as the disciples were crossing the Sea of Galilee in a boat. They wondered, "What manner of man is this that even the winds and the waves obey Him?!"

What manner of man was He? Well, He had a commanding presence, but not as General Patton did. His wasn't the self-confident posture of a person who stands before the American flag that symbolizes the huge self-confidence of the United States of America with its bomber jets, nuclear submarines, guided missiles, and army with extravagant destructive capacity.

His was a commanding presence that could receive the taunts, indecencies, and tortures of crude Roman soldiers and say compassionately, "Father forgive them for they know not what they do." His was a commanding presence that could receive a woman caught in an act that goaded some religious men to want to stone her to death for her irreligious behavior, and at once let them sense their impropriety, and this woman feel loved, accepted, and of unspeakable value to God. He spoke to them one sentence whose sting was applied to each by each one's self-perception of guilt, perhaps without looking up while, all the while doodling in the dust. He let these men know that the moment of their zeal for God's law that their passion was a sham.

When I think of the Lordship of Jesus, I remember all these things. But Jesus' lordship that we claim to believe has claims on my life and yours that are quite specific. It is a claim on us we either receive voluntarily now or not at all now. Jesus doesn't impose His lordship on us. The words of invitation, that I will remind you of again in just a few minutes as we take to us the common sacred elements of bread and wine Jesus taught us to receive, were the words Jesus used to invite Peter and Andrew, James and John to be His disciples when he saw them fishing. Jesus' invitation is always, "Come to me, all who are weary and heavy laden, and I will give you rest."

We should not imagine that Jesus summons people to His lordship as Uncle Sam commands young men to join the military, or Notre Dame recruits football players— trying to find the strongest, the fastest, the bravest, and the nimblest young men to make its team as dominant as possible. Jesus didn't summon Peter and Andrew, James and John, or you and me because He needed us to make His team successful. He summoned us to Him to give us rest, and at the same time to extend His work of bringing healing to the world.

He said, "Take my yoke on you." He said, "Come, learn from me."

And this part of His invitation is no less significant than His comforting words, "Come all who are weary." But the former words have somehow been muted. Customarily we'd prefer to come to Jesus "who knows our every weakness."

I read this week the New York Times' review of Lawrence Friedman's book, *Crime and Punishment in American History*. A quote from his book leaped out at me. "The present century became the century of the self, the century of expressive individualism. This new concept of self lies behind the women's movement, the civil rights movement, the sexual revolution. But the culture of rampant individualism has its dark side: A great deal of 20th-century crime can be explained, if at all, in terms of the exaltation of the self, a 20th-century pathology."

By contrast, the Apostle Paul showed us what makes Christianity tick when he said, "For me to live is Christ." It is true that Jesus said, "I came that you may have life and have it more abundantly," but He didn't then, advise you to plead, "Let me be me."

You and I show what is making Christianity sputter every time we say, "Let me be me." Every time you and I insist on our own way; every time we think or say, "Don't tell me what I must do," we are simply showing how well we fit into Friedman's assessment of the 20th-century pathology.

Jesus wants to rescue you and me from this pathology. No one who has accepted deeply His lordship has found Him a heavy taskmaster. But He will command us to forgive people we may not want to forgive. And in doing so He will remove a possible cause of our heart attacks. He will command us to share significantly of what we think we "own" with others, a distribution that will bring us joy in doing it. He will command us to love people whom we instinctively shy away from, but this too will give us delight. He will command us to be bold in saying we trust in Him, but modest in projecting any arrogance in doing so, as though to despise those who do not.

Jesus' lordship will mean we will forget to ask, "what's in it for me?" while asking persistently, "What will bring glory to God and good for other people." You and I don't accept Jesus' lordship to get eternal life, or even to receive "God's wonderful plan for our lives." These may come as a result, but they are not the motive if Jesus is "Lord" rather than the Divine means to our happy ends.

There is another aspect to this that I don't want to mention with any harshness, but it is there, and it is a solemn thing to recognize. One day every knee will bow before Him, in heaven and on earth, and under the earth—which means people from all ages of history as well as angels. Every tongue will confess that Jesus Christ is Lord, to the glory of God the Father.

That seems a long way off, maybe so far away as to seem an illusion. When you were a child, you looked at getting married in a similar way. If you are in high school, you look at having a career in somewhat the same way. But then the day comes when we suddenly realize we stand with our beloved before a pastor, and we are dressed in our best to hear the words, "I now pronounce you husband and wife." The day comes also when we realize we've got to now get up every morning and go to work. And the day will come when you and I will discover that we are standing in the presence of a gracious God, who gave us so much opportunity to accept His grace-laden lordship in life.

The psalms tell us that God's mercies are everlasting. Paul tells us that nothing can separate us from the love of God in Christ Jesus our Lord.

Try to imagine a life freed from the insatiable, undefined, unachievable quest of self-fulfillment, so that we discovered the joyous life for which we were created—under the loving lordship of Jesus.

Let us pray: Thank you, gracious Lord God, Creator of heaven and earth and of all things seen and unseen, that you gave to us Your

Only Son, born of the Virgin Mary. We thank you for the amazing spectacle of His Lordship then, and for the kindly invitation He has offered us still to come to Him to find rest. Oh, give us a heart to follow Him, to accept His light yoke. Free us from the shackles of our selfishness, to find perfect freedom in His service. For Jesus' sake, Amen.

He was Conceived by the Holy Ghost, Born of the Virgin Mary
Isaiah 7:10-17; Luke 1:26-35

Every time we say the Creed we say we believe Jesus "was conceived by the Holy Ghost, born of the Virgin Mary." But, usually it is only near Christmas, the time when we celebrate the birth of Jesus, that you hear someone read the story in Luke that tells us the angel's surprising message to the Virgin Mary. "You're going to have a son by a special act of the Holy Spirit!"

Daunted, Mary asked how she could have a son since she wasn't even married.

The Angel Gabriel tells her: "The Holy Spirit will come upon you, and the power of the Most High will overshadow you, therefore the child to be born will be called holy, the Son of God."

The other Gospel that tells us about this extraordinary birth, Matthew, lets us know that Joseph, the man to whom Mary was engaged, at least toyed with the idea of not going through with marrying her. He knew he hadn't sired that child growing in her womb; how could he believe her story about the angel's message? But an angel told him that Mary wasn't making this story up. "That which is conceived in her is of the Holy Spirit. This is a fulfillment of Isaiah's prophecy, 'Behold a virgin shall conceive and bear a son'." So, Joseph stayed with Mary, trusting her, no matter what others thought. He was a just and fair man.

The teaching of the New Testament about how Jesus began His life wasn't accepted by everyone in early Christianity. Some of the early Christians denied that Jesus' origin was different from that of any other man, no matter what the Gospels said. Joseph was Jesus' father, they said, just as Irvine was mine, or Thomas, James, or William was yours.

Many moderns choke at this too. When I was in seminary, I think I was the only one in the Isaiah course, where we studied the Old Testament reading for this morning, who believed that Isaiah 7 really foretold the Virgin birth of Jesus. Let me discuss this passage somewhat technically.

For one thing, it was pointed out quite rightly that Isaiah 7:14 in the language Isaiah wrote, Hebrew, really reads, "a young woman **has conceived** and will bear a child" rather than "a virgin **shall** conceive and bear a son." The one little word translated "has conceived" is an adjective that means "pregnant." It is the Greek translation of the Old Testament that Matthew is quoting, and the Greek uses the specific word for "virgin," and changes the tense from past to future in this place.

Unless I am mistaken, this is the only place in the Greek Bible where the Greek word for "virgin" translates the Hebrew word for "young woman." The King James Version English translation of the word "young woman" is also translated "virgin" in three other places; once in Genesis and twice in the Song of Solomon, but these are the translator's decision of the young women referred to are virgins. Just that. In Hebrew there is another word that specifically means "virgin." If you search Strong's or Young's concordances, you will see the Hebrew word for "virgin" referred to numerous times, forty-six, in fact, by my count.

Young unmarried women, of course, in ancient Israel were virgins, but if this young woman was pregnant, she was not then a virgin—unless some cause otherwise unknown induced her pregnancy. The law required the Jews to treat unmarried young women who engaged in sexual activity severely. The virgin in this place did not violate any moral law because she had not yet conceived. She would conceive in the future and give birth to a son.

The translators of the Hebrew Bible into Greek were Jews who had no theological agenda; they weren't aware of the event that would happen many years later involving Jesus' birth to a peasant Virgin from Nazareth.

The earliest translation of the Hebrew Bible was into Aramaic, the language the Jews learned in exile. It is a close relative of Hebrew. The written form of these Aramaic translations are called Targums. The Targum of Isaiah 7: 14 translates the Hebrew word with an

Aramaic word meaning the same thing. It comes from a root meaning "strong" and only means a young woman.

As Joseph would have heard Isaiah 7 expounded in the synagogue, perhaps the rabbi would have explained the sense of this young woman as a virgin, because her conception was to be a divine sign that Isaiah was telling King Ahaz. And it is perhaps for this reason that the Greek translation of the one Hebrew word meaning "young woman" is "virgin." For a virgin to conceive must be a divine sign. That the time of the coming of the sign should be changed from the present to the future may be because the sign was not yet; it was yet to come.

Why is the special conception of Jesus important for us moderns to believe?

Why should we accept the notion that only ancient peoples could believe such a thing? I'm reminded of Chesterton's remark about things that were quite credible hundreds of years ago that aren't believable today. "You might as well say that a certain philosophy can be believed on Mondays but cannot be believed on Tuesdays. . . that it was suitable to half-past three, but not suitable to half-past four." We're not talking about something that can be proved or disproved by modern scientific evidence. We're talking about something that many ancients found unbelievable because it was just as much beyond their experience as it is ours.

Let us be clear in acknowledging that Jesus was born of a Virgin, by a special act of the Holy Spirit, not because there is anything evil about sex. God invented sex, you remember. It's completely His idea. God could have used the usual way babies are conceived, had He so chosen.

The Virgin birth was not necessary because Jesus was half-God and half-man, or not really a human. We should not imagine the New Testament is teaching us there was some sort of sexual union between God, the Holy Spirit, and Mary in the way Mesopotamian, Greek, and Roman deities consorted with humans sexually. Jesus was fully a man just as I am. But he was also fully God as none of us people are. I believe Jesus was born of a virgin simply to underscore the fact of this new thing God did in Jesus. Furthermore, Jesus' Virgin birth would become an illustration of a truth best illustrated for us in this way. It is a mystery with a purpose.

The Apostle Paul explains to us that Jesus Christ was a second Adam. "The first Adam became a living being, the last Adam became a life-giving spirit" (I Corinthians 15.45). The first Adam came into being by a special act of God; the second Adam came into being by a special act of God. As in the first Adam, all die, so in Christ, the second Adam, shall all be made alive" (I Cor. 15:52). This is a teaching that doesn't lend itself too well to the biologist's or geneticist's genius to explain.

John's Gospel, which does not describe the virgin birth, tells us that if you and I have "received" Jesus, something similar has happened in us. When Jesus explained this to Nicodemas he did not understand. In fact, it's not clear that he ever understood. "How can a person enter the mother's womb and be born again?" Jesus' answer didn't answer that question. His answer, however, described something else that we perceive regularly that we don't understand either; where and how a wind that we can feel begins.

John writes: "To all who received him, who believed in his name, God gave the power to become children of God, who were born, not of blood, nor of the will of the flesh nor of the will of man, but of God" (John 1:12-13). The language in which the Gospel writer wrote has it, ". . . who were born not of bloods," rather than "not of blood." When you and I were conceived there was the mingling of bloods, so to speak, the bloods of our mother and father. But when we receive Christ our faith is the result of a special act of the Holy Spirit in our hearts as Jesus' birth was the result of a special act of the Holy Spirit in Mary's body. It borders on sacrilege to try to explain this, but I think we are to understand that when we are born "from above," or "again," it is a work of God as it was a Divine impulse by which Jesus was conceived in His virgin mother.

Maybe you haven't thought of your faith in Jesus in this way. Faith in Jesus is not "mere belief," the kind of belief you have in "facts" you read in books. Faith in Jesus, as the Heidelberg Catechism reminds us, "is a whole-hearted trust which the Holy Spirit creates in me through the Gospel" (Question 21). It begins like the wind.

Zealous Americans don't take kindly to citizens who burn flags, degrade their country, or who otherwise take this privilege of citizenship lightly.

But we may take our citizenship in heaven, as children of God, lightly, perhaps on a par with our citizenship on earth.

When you and I received diplomas after being welcomed into various levels of academic achievement, our diplomas told us something to the effect that we were "entitled to all the rights, privileges, honors and marks of distinction thereto pertaining here or elsewhere." We had colorful hoods put on us that we understood meant that we were to "wear" our degrees in such a way that we brought distinction to the institution that awarded them.

This is very modestly like our responsibility as people who have believed in Jesus. Jesus invited us to come to Him. You and I are named by His title, Christ. We are "Christians."

We follow Him in being "born again" by an act of the Spirit of God as He was born by an act of the Spirit of God. We are to follow Him in being committed to doing the will of God as He was. We are assured we will follow Him in being raised from death.

I wonder if you have considered how high an honor it is to be called a Christian.

Still God graciously assures us that if we believe we have followed Him in our Holy Spirit-conceived new birth, and we will follow Him in being raised from death.

I've been reading C.S. Lewis' *Mere Christianity* with a new friend over the past few weeks. He and I have noticed what a difference there is between really doing what following Jesus means, and merely living as Christians most often live.

Where do we derive our ideas of what it means to live as a Christian? Have we learned badly from too much watching inadequate examples? What about taking to heart Jesus' loving invitation, "Come to me ... take my yoke on you and learn of me?" After all, if we are "in Christ," we have been "born again" by the same Spirit who brought about our birth.

When we say we believe Jesus was "conceived by the Holy Ghost, born of the Virgin Mary," we are claiming our birthright as much as His. I appeal to you, as I strive myself, to live up to the birthright we have with Jesus.

Let us pray: "Lord God, we believe with gratitude your Word that informs us of Jesus' special birth to the Virgin Mary. We thank you that we have been "born again to a living hope by the resurrection of Jesus from death." Grant to us your Holy Spirit to polish and finish that recreating work He began in us, so that when our Lord Jesus returns, He and we may be delighted at His coming. We pray through Jesus Christ, our Lord, Amen.

He Suffered under Pontius Pilate
Isaiah 53:1-12; John 19:1-16

We have arrived at a statement in the Apostles' Creed which any reasonable person must consider truly awful. It goads me to do some deep thinking.

Of this One who had such a beginning of life we abruptly say, "He suffered under Pontius Pilate. We usually say this without crying—the starkness escapes us. I think maybe the one good effect of Mel Gibson's movie, "The Passion of Christ," is that it depicted Jesus' suffering so thoroughly that I could not keep from crying. I was not the only one that cried in the theater, though I saw some people eating popcorn.

There is a yawning gap between Jesus' conception and birth and His death. We say the Creed as though Jesus had no childhood, no life in between. No miracles, no call to twelve disciples, no teachings, or even an exemplary life. Why were the early Christian teachers so crass as to think we should remember only Jesus' birth, suffering, death, and what happened afterwards—and nothing at all about His life?

I'm reminded of something I read recently in the *New York Times*, in which the writer remarked on the tragedy that we know nothing about most people until they die. Then we know about them because their names are introduced to us in an obituary.

In the obituary we may read some innocuous headlines that narrow all their lives' meaning down to how they earned money, or how they liked to spend their leisure. We don't think ill of the editor for these reductions of the significance of these people because she never knew about these persons before. What else could she write except? — "John Doe retired from Eli Lilly," or "Jane Doe taught at Purdue." Or maybe, "he loved to go bowling and was well liked." The deceased person's relatives report these often-innocuous details because the funeral director asks them what they would like the obituary to say, as they go about the grim task of choosing a coffin. The event that draws our notice is not really where he or she worked, but that she died. After her tiny birth announcement long ago, she never drew a public comment in a newspaper until her death announcement.

The Apostles' Creed seems guilty of an even greater reduction of Jesus' life—it doesn't tell us where and how Jesus worked in the small towns of Galilee, or about His walks on the dusty roads in between where He met and engaged people whose lives were changed by their encounter with Jesus. They sat in the dust blind until Jesus touched their eyes. Life immediately changed. They could see.

Jesus was born miraculously, and then he died with great suffering. That's all. Wasn't His life important? Shouldn't we say we believe something more about this great Teacher, this supreme Lover of humanity, this unparalleled Miracle-worker?

I was once asked why the Creed includes Jesus suffering under Pontius Pilate. It might have told us of Jesus' trial before the High Priest, and the role of those who said, "Crucify Him."

There is no anti-Semitism in the Creed. Jesus could have summoned twelve legions of angels for His defense, Matthew writes, but He didn't. The only angels that took part in the three-day span of Jesus' final days' physical presence on earth stood witness to His resurrection at the tomb.

As crass as it might seem, The Apostles' Creed has said the most important things about Jesus' life. Jesus was born to suffer and die for us. His life was wonderful and important, of course. But had He not suffered and died for us, He would not have been more important to us than any other great teacher who lived, taught, and died. Socrates' unmerited death has sometimes been compared in its nobility to Jesus' death. He too was accused of heretical beliefs. But Socrates' lingering benefit had nothing to do with addressing the mystery of life's great longing for meaning beyond the grave.

John 3:16 tells us, "For God so loved the world that He gave His Only Son that whoever believes in Him will have eternal life." When John writes, "He gave His Only Son," he puts it into a five-word capsule Jesus' life's odyssey from His birth through His ascension, leaving out all the details in between. Here is what is uniquely important for us to know and believe: God gave us His Only Son to suffer and to die for us.

Let us not belittle the importance of Jesus' teachings, or of His good deeds, or all that He did for people that had great need. But no one can follow Jesus' example closely enough for His mere life's example to do them as much good as they need. The glaring weakness of the kind of Christianity that merely emphasizes these exemplary aspects of Jesus' life is that it does so at the expense of taking fully to heart that Jesus came to suffer and die for our sins.

How we idolize noble people, and rightly so. We owe much to our Abraham Lincolns and Mother Teresas as models of virtue. I hope we may be influenced by their noble examples. But very many folks stumble at the idea that we needed someone to suffer and die for us because of our sin. The Gospel, the Good News is that not only did we need someone to suffer and die for us to secure for us eternal life with God, but that Someone did suffer and die for us—the only One who could.

I also think this tells us something about what was important to God for God's sake. He did not create us in His image and likeness just to dispose of us in a place of refuse called "*hades*" (the place of the dead) when "things didn't work out." He created us for fellowship with Him, so that He needed to reconcile us to Himself to resume this "camaraderie," which I hope is not too flippant an idea. Part of the message of the Gospel is that immediately after Jesus' began His ministry, He gathered a circle of friends. These were to be the first installment, so to speak, of an ever-widening circle of friends. As Abraham was first called a "friend of God," so it is God's ambition that we be His friends too.

The most important thing the early Christians believed the prophet Isaiah wrote about Jesus was: he was despised and rejected, a man of sorrows, acquainted with grief. He was wounded for our transgressions, bruised for our iniquities. . .by His stirpes we are healed." He wrote other things about him – about His opening the eyes of the blind and causing the lame to leap like deer— but this was the most important of all because the purpose this suffering achieved.

Christians noticed that in Isaiah 50 the prophet seems to depict Jesus' suffering on the cross. "I gave my back to the smiters, and my cheeks to those that pulled out the beard; I hid not my face from shame and spitting" (50: 6). Psalm 22 is like Jesus script for what He would say on the cross. But what we should most notice is not these interesting allusions to what took place in Jesus' passion, but the reason why he suffered and died.

Today I have emphasized that the Creed reminds us of what we learn from Isaiah and read in the Gospels that Jesus' death was accompanied by suffering for our sake. Why was this detail of suffering so important to include in the Creed?

I'm not sure I know any complete answer to this, but from what I can see, the story of humanity, that began so well, was not only undermined by sin, and cut short by death, but became cluttered with suffering. Somehow all this suffering itself needed to be healed. God, who created everything good grieves at the suffering in the world.

I speak with widows and feel their huge lingering sense of loss. Mary Lou Varys' mother just became a widow on Saturday. I was just reminded again of the sorrow of widows. How can we tabulate the sum of all the sorrow people have endured at the untimely death of loved ones?!

I read of the Jewish Holocaust and I am numb. I visited Auschwitz a few years ago and seemed to feel the lingering sense of the terror of the place. So much cruelty dealt to human beings by human beings. Hatred presided there. I look at the present agonies in Somalia, Liberia, and Bosnia and I ache. One of my students at Purdue, a young nursing student from Liberia, called me this week all distraught. Her father's brother was just shot and killed on Monday. The civil war there has become worse. Her parents are in danger and she can do nothing about it. What could I say as she wept in telling me these things? Civil wars produce unspeakable cruelties of brother against brother. They always have.

Before we worshipped last Sunday, just down the road from us four young men were killed in a car crash.

The list of sufferings in our world keeps growing.

One of the early Church fathers, Irenaeus, taught us that Jesus' ministry to us recapitulated or summed up life as we live it. He was a child in order that He might redeem children. He became a young man to redeem young people. He became an adult to save adults. And He suffered to heal the suffering of the world.

One further thing strikes me about this suffering. Suffering introduces people to profound loneliness.

Ultimately, people suffer alone. When Jesus suffered, He was alone; forsaken by all His friends. He took on Himself the aloneness as well as the pain of our suffering.

The Bible and the Creed underscore Jesus' solitary suffering in telling us that He was by Himself in Pontius Pilate judgment hall. Neither His mother, nor any of Jesus' friends, were with Him. Pilate was a frightening man. The awfulness and loneliness of Jesus is accentuated when we know how solitary was this moment before Pilate. The Creed tells us the names of only three people: Mary, Jesus, and Pilate. Why is unholy Pilate listed alongside of holy Mary, Blessed among women, and Holy Jesus, God's only Son, our Lord? Did so bad a man deserve a place in sacred history?

Yes. Because in telling us that such a wicked man-made Jesus suffer we can know that Jesus' understood the depths of possible suffering.

I think many people have some idea of what Pilate was like from watching "Ben Hur" or Hollywood's other depictions of Jesus' story. Josephus makes plain that Pilate's ten years over the Jews was one of the worst blemishes of the Roman occupation of Judea.

The Gospels seem to be compassionate toward Pilate, as though they reflect Jesus' own compassion for those who made Him suffer. Why did Pilate have to be the governor of Judea at that moment? You remember Jesus said from the cross, "Father forgive them for they know not what they do." Who was this anonymous "them?" Was Pilate too included in this sum of ignorant people?

Reflecting Jesus' compassion, John's Gospel tells us that Pilate felt himself over his head in being forced to judge Jesus. He was frightened. Matthew tells us that Pilate, a man capable of immense injustice without blushing, was sick at heart with Jesus before him. Why else did he washed his hands symbolically, as though by washing his hands he was released of any complicity in Jesus' death? What could he do to ceremonially, as it were, rid himself of responsibility for what happened to Jesus. His wife had told him to have nothing to do with this just man (27:19). How much he would have liked to be able to follow her advice. But he did not. He let his soldiers inflict insults and injuries on Jesus before crucifying Him.

Why do we need to know all this, and to believe it? Because we need to realize that God really understood our need—that we not only could find forgiveness for our sins, but that we can find healing for our suffering. Only by identifying fully with the depths of human aloneness in suffering could God heal this awful ache in the world. When God sent His Only Son into the world, He sent Him to experience the depths of human need. Paul tells us that "He who knew no sin, became sin for us." The Gospels show us that He who had known only heaven's bliss endured the extremes of human suffering.

Just now, it would seem, neither the sin nor the ache of the world has been healed. You might well say that someone who is suffering now finds little consolation in knowing that Jesus or anyone else suffered. But the hope of the Gospel is that what we see or feel now is not the end of the story. Just as mothers who suffer in labor forget the pains of child birth after they hold their little ones in their arms, so we will all understand the goodness of God in due time.

We may believe that Jesus' death for our sins was effective. After all, you can't see or feel sin. We see sins, but never as God does, so we trust that when the Bible tells us God forgives our sins, it is so. But probably there is no aspect of our faith that is more difficult to grasp now than to believe that Jesus' suffering for us provided the cure for our pain. Here, too, we must trust that it is so. It is part of the hope of the Gospel.

Finally, lest we think too much merely about our own needs, and our yearning to see suffering end, I must remind myself and you all, that Jesus suffered for us, not because of how evil Pontius Pilate was, but because we, you and I, imposed this on Him too. Rembrandt painted a picture of the crucifixion in which he displays in the foreground all the customary people who were part of that scene—the soldiers, the scoffing religious leaders. But you can, if you look closely, see in the shadows another figure which is Rembrandt himself. Here the great painter testifies the same thing that Charles Wesley admitted in his great hymn: "He died for me who caused His pain." "Amazing love, how can it be, that Thou my God should'st die for me!"

I do not say this to add any guilt to your sufferings, but only to try to ignite in you thanks to God that His grace reaches out through our suffering. Put your present sufferings into the bigger picture and trust that God, who has demonstrated His love and His power so well, will prove to you in due time that He loves you as you need most to be loved. "All will be well, and all manner of things will be well," as Julian of Norwich told us long ago.

Let us pray: "Lord God, we understand so little about our suffering. We only wish it would go away. We seldom listen well to how you whisper to us in our pain to draw near to you. We thank you that Jesus suffered for us, that He knows how suffering hurts, and that He will heal us. We wait with eagerness for the time when all suffering will end, when we see Jesus face to face. Give us grace and wisdom to live with this joyful day ever in our thoughts. For Jesus' sake, Amen.

He Was Crucified, Dead, and Buried
Psalm 69:1-21; Matthew 27:27-44

We began our worship this morning singing that triumphant hymn: "Lift High the Cross." How enthusiastically you sang this hymn! The cross is a very popular symbol today. If we were to take an inventory of the jewelry you are wearing this morning, I would guess we would find some crosses.

But it symbolizes what the psalmist wrote, "More in number than the hairs of my head are those who hate me without cause . . . I have become a stranger to my brethren, an alien to my mother's sons."

This morning I want to lead you to consider again the cross. The Creed tells us, "Jesus was crucified, dead, and buried." In this threefold declaration, it emphasizes that the reason for which Jesus was born was fulfilled. It answers the charge of some in the early and recent Church that the son of God did not really die on the cross. He was drugged and came to life afterwards. It itemizes the stages of His end: He was crucified (a cruel punishment that always ended in death); He died; He was buried. Let there be no mistake. What does this mean for us?

I want to think with you about two signs of this cross of Jesus. First, there is the usual figure you have in mind, and second there is another important symbol you may not have in mind when you think of the cross of Jesus.

First, then, is the usual figure of the cross. Why do we sing of the cross? Do we lift high this sign because Christianity won in the religious struggles of the ancient world? It can look like a conquering sword, with a short handle, a long blade, and a cross piece to protect the hand of the one that wields it. Is the prevalence of the cross a testimony to Emperor Constantine's triumph at the Battle of Milvian Bridge before which he claimed to have seen a vision of the first two letters of the word Christ?

Christianity indeed "won" in the religious conflict of the ancient world, and Constantine played no small role in this victory, but I think I see a triumphalism in the popular use of the cross that contradicts the real victory of the cross. The cross didn't win in the way General Schwartzkopf won in Operation Desert Storm. Jesus' triumph on the cross was not followed by a ticker-tape parade. That came the week before and the throngs who waved their palms weren't aware of what was in the works. The cross is not a symbol on a pennant to wave against the pennants of other religions the way you might wave a Purdue pennant before a football game against Indiana University. Ought the cross to be waved or worn proudly the way we wave and wear the American flag?

The victory of the cross was a rather unique victory, unlike most victories we lovers of winning love to celebrate.

I wonder if, despite this, there is something quite right about the popularity of the cross because the cross is central to the Christian Gospel. Sometimes we don't fully know what we're cheering for. We're correct and right, but not as we imagine.

The Apostle Paul calls the Gospel, "the word of the cross which is foolishness" (I Cor. 1:18). The Gospel is not the winning word that you can be all you were meant to be, or any of those slogans that many people like to hear today in church. It's true that Jesus came to give us "an abundant life," but this may not be the same thing as "abundant life."

In a way, the Gospel offers the very opposite of this. For this we should be glad because the one we see in the mirror will pass away soon, while the victory we have in the cross will last forever.

This morning we will remember the cross in another sign, the sacrament of Baptism. The psalm Jurgen Honig read for us this morning has been read by Christians for centuries as a psalm of the cross because it describes so pathetically the experience of Jesus on the cross. Verse 21 reads, "For my thirst they gave me vinegar to drink."

Our New Testament reading, Matthew 27:48, points us back to this verse— "And one of them at once ran and took a sponge, filled it with vinegar, and gave it to him to drink."

I doubt that the psalmist was thinking about Baptism when he wrote, but notice, how Psalm 69 begins: "Save me, O God! For the waters have come up to my neck ... I have come into deep waters, and the flood sweeps over me." Water figures prominently in the Bible's teaching about how God saves us. But the waters are not friendly. They are not like the refreshing water in a swimming pool.

In I Peter 3:20, the apostle points us back to the days of Noah who was "saved through water." This water brought death to a sinful generation, but life to Noah and his family. Peter goes on to write: "Baptism, which corresponds to this, now saves you, . . . as an appeal to God for a clear conscience, through the resurrection of Jesus Christ."

The early Church teachers also liked to point to the opening of the Red Sea for the Israelites as they escaped from there. Egyptian bondage as a symbol of death; here God saved His people through water.

In all this imagery death is closely tied in with salvation, that is, life. A whole generation died but Noah and his family were saved.

An Egyptian army of charioteers died when Israel was given life through the Red Sea. This too is part of the Christian sacrament of Baptism but not quite as we might think.

The Apostle Paul wrote, "Do you not know that all of us who have been baptized into Christ Jesus were baptized into his 'death" (Rom. 6:3)? I would guess we seldom think of this at baptism. It is difficult to connect all these ideas. Is it indeed a baptism into Jesus' death?

When we baptize little Barbara Elizabeth, it will be the inaugural moment in her life of faith. Her parents claim for her their covenant they have made with God. It is difficult to think of the cruelty of the cross, or if the drowning of multitudes in Noah's day, or of Egyptian soldiers that pursued the Israelites at the Exodus. She is too small, and cute. We associate the baptism of infants much more with the promise of life. I lift her in my arms and carry her about for you to see. You will smile and applaud, welcoming her into the Church.

But the truth is still there. Little Barbara Elizabeth is being identified with the cross. We are claiming for her the work of the Holy Spirit to convince her to believe when she is old enough to understand that Jesus' death on the cross was for her. When adults are baptized, it is important for them to understand this as they are baptized.

We aren't told of the Apostle Paul's baptism, but he must have been baptized. I think this is what he thought as he was baptized., "I have been crucified with Christ; it is no longer I who live, but Christ who lives in me; and the life I now live in the flesh I live by faith in the Son of God, who loved me and gave himself for me" (Gal. 2:20). We aren't told he was baptized, but it certainly fits such a moment in his life.

The way baptism was done originally, a manner that is practiced today in some churches, it may have been easier to understand this idea. The person being baptized was put completely beneath the water; it was a symbolic drowning. The whole body from the top of the head to the tippy toes, went under. Why? Because it was a visual symbol of the complete identification with Christ's death. There was some humiliation as the person was unclad to receive baptism. As Job put it, "naked I came from my mother's womb; and naked I shall I return" (Job 1: 21). We are too proper to accept the full symbolism of baptism. After coming up from the water a white cloth was put around him. The person unwittingly was claiming for herself Job's words. In some of the earlier days of Christian history, when it was not so safe to be a Christian it was easier to understand, "I have been buried with Him in baptism" (Rom. 6:4). As the psalmist wrote, "I have come into deep waters, and the flood sweeps over me." It is a symbol of dying.

How should we respond to Jesus' cross if it is so central to our faith, its death the archetype of baptism?

When I began to think about this morning's sermon, I wondered if I should tell you of a physician's account I read of what happened to a person's body in being crucified, of how excruciating was the agony of crucifixion. Is this what we should really think about the most?

We preachers are tempted to think that if only everyone appreciated how badly it hurt when Jesus was crucified, this would prompt us all to be "better Christians." But I chose not to go this route because Jesus does not want us to sit forever staring at the picture of Him on the cross. I don't quite know what to think of the Gospel song, "The Old Rugged Cross," which makes it almost seem like a beloved old car kept for sentimental reasons in the barn.

We're tempted to another line of response to the cross. When we sing the hymn "When I Survey the Wondrous Cross," and come to those words, "See from His head, His hands, His feet, sorrow and love flow mingled down," I can scarcely repress the instinct that makes my throat choke. I often tear up. I agree then with Isaac Watts' testimony, "Love so amazing, so divine, demands my soul, my life, my all." It is true, "Were the whole realm of nature mine, that were a present far too small. Love so amazing, so divine, demands my soul, my life, my all."

But Jesus never told us, "One good turn deserves another."

Jesus did not die for you and me to force us to a return favor. There is not a trace of *quid pro quo* in the message of the Gospel. We can't pay Jesus back. I know the sentiment of the song, "Jesus paid it all; all to Him I owe." But it is a bit off target.

Why? For one thing, we have nothing that can compare with the gift of the Son of God for us. Furthermore, this motivation doesn't work. The quality of Christianity that tries to pay Jesus back for what He did for us has often been morbid. Earnest Christians have inflicted pain on themselves as a way of paying Jesus back, as though this did any good at all. Martin Luther as a young monk thought about the cross and beat his own back with thongs until he became unconscious. His tender spiritual father told him, "Brother Martin, this isn't what Jesus asks of you." If, during Lent, you deny yourself anything as a means of paying Jesus back, you've missed the point. If you do good deeds for others, or if you go to church, or if you give your money to charitable causes as a means of paying Jesus back, you've missed the point.

What then does Jesus' crucifixion mean for us? First, it simply means that when Jesus died, it was God's plan that this was how your sin and mine should be punished. Jesus bore in His body on the cross your sin and mine. What we deserve for our sin—and we all sin—is death. Jesus died so that we would not need to die for our sin. All we can do is to say thank you and accept it.

The humility you feel when you realize that all you can do is to believe and to say, "thank you" is appropriate. The most suitable response any of us can have to the cross is first to humbly feel gratitude. It was for me that Jesus died.

But if we are truly grateful, we want to go beyond saying thank you. If we rightly understand how central the cross of Jesus is to the Gospel we believe, we must accept for ourselves Jesus' attitude on the cross. Paul wrote, "Let this mind be in you, which is yours in Christ Jesus."

When we say we are following Jesus, we are not simply claiming to follow His teachings. For sure we're not paying Him back or rewarding Him with the gift of our lives. It is the Jesus that we see on the cross that is our most insistent model. In a way, the Christian faith is taking on the unfinished task begun when Jesus humbled Himself and accepted death on the cross; it awaits those of us who say we believe in Him.

Somehow this is an aspect of the Gospel that has become lost and replaced by other goals. I am puzzled at the capacity for hostility and pride in Christianity. Where has the adversarial spirit come from that has Christians competing with one another, belittling and accusing one another of inadequacies? I see some churches advertising themselves as though there were some ultimate value to being part of their triumphant movement. What about the Cross prompts this? How uncompetitive Jesus was hanging there! How unappealing as a model for success! Who wants the kind of triumph Jesus seemed to stand for there?

I see Christians competing with other religions for converts and know that in doing so they may say hostile things about their competitors. We count converts the way politicians count votes. Should Christians be impolite to Mormon missionaries, often idealistic, fine young folk that give two years of their lives to spreading the religion they think is the right one? When the Jehovah's Witnesses come to your door are you polite, appreciating their faithfulness to their cause? Remember how the Jesus who went to the cross spoke with a pagan centurion and a Samaritan outcast. How gracious He was.

What is the prompting for the angry response of Christians to cultural sins?

Surely not from the Jesus they see on the cross. When you see certain kinds of behavior in society that you think must be corrected, is the victory you want over that behavior informed by the kind of victory you watched Jesus achieve on the cross? When I see the Right to Life Movement's rage against those who do abortions, or when I see Christians agitate for displaying the Ten Commandments or Christmas scenes on courthouse lawns, I wonder what it is about taking up Jesus cross that motivates this. We have yet to learn Jesus' victory tactics on the cross.

I wonder if you were to see Jesus clearly looking down at His tormentors, praying, "Father forgive them, for they know not what they do," and remember this when you are being tormented by your brother or sister or neighbor or boss, would your response to him or her be the same as it naturally is? When you think of people in this congregation who bug you, is your response to them informed by the Jesus you see on the cross?

You may respond by thinking that Jesus' manner of victory was far too passive for the real world. You will certainly recognize that Jesus' victory on the cross constricts the instincts in you that want to express themselves. And so, you will want to argue with me about this.

But let me remind you, when you say you believe Jesus was crucified, you acknowledge that He was obedient even to death on the cross for you. He won a grim victory for you in that death. It was a victory that you and I are called on to win over the world too. By the same kind of means it is a victory of grace.

I read of an Anglican Bishop in Vermont, much beloved by his people, who died. After he died his nurse said to a friend, "I know where the Bishop is tonight. His soul has gone to hell." The friend was shocked, but the nurse went on: "That's the only place he can be happy; there's such work to do there."

This was Jesus' spirit. He sought out hell--the hell of the cross, so that by His defeat there He could win something that only this defeat could win for you and me. Jesus says to us-- "Come, follow me." Ought we then to go as Jesus did to where He went? We will think about this next.

Let us pray: Lord God, we are very thankful Jesus went to the cross for us. We hear His call: "Come, follow me." But everything in us conspires to misunderstand this call. We want to win, not to lose. Oh, give to us your Holy Spirit to explain to us deeply how to follow Jesus. Help me to cherish the cross of Jesus, and to be willing to carry my own cross--that I may reign with Him, in the way Jesus reigns. We pray in Jesus' name. Amen.

He Descended into Hell
II Samuel 22:1-20 Ephesians 4:1-10

Some of you already noticed last week the interesting coincidence that on Halloween I proposed to speak on the topic before us today. I assure you I never planned this; it just happened—providentially, I might say appropriately, since we Presbyterians are heirs of John Calvin. I remind you that today is not only Halloween, but also the day on which we remember that Martin Luther fired the salvo that awoke the Western Church to the truth of the Grace of God. I hope today this grace will become even more beautiful and winsome to you.

King David composed a song of deliverance that found a place in the Bible not only in II Samuel but also in the Book of Psalms (18). In II Samuel this song follows David's defeat of four Philistine giants after a struggle that must have left him spiritually as well as physically exhausted. These giants were not just very tall men. Their giant stature was accompanied by a super-human quality. They may have been related to the giants mentioned in Genesis 6, whose parents mingled in them super-human and human genes.

He wrote, "The waves of death encompassed me, the torrents of perdition assailed me; the cords of Sheol entangled me, the snares of death confronted me." It was for him a "dark night of the soul." He had to repeat four times the depths of his distress to signify its extent: death, perdition, Sheol, and finally death again. This is echoed in Psalm 116: 3.

Perhaps there are those of you that resonate with what he writes. Calvin referred to the psalms as offering "an anatomy of all the parts of the soul."

Many of us have faced moments so painful that they seemed to make of life a living hell. Not a few people afflicted with bi-polar mental illness feel, in their lowest times, dread deeper than fear. A clinical depression can impose lingering, unbearable mental misery. Did Paul write of this in Ephesians 4: 9, that before Jesus ascended to the Father, "he descended into the lower parts of the earth?" When Jesus sweat blood in the Garden of Gethsemane, was it of such a time that Paul wrote? I wonder if the writer is describing this in Hebrews 2, that Jesus was a "pioneer in suffering, being made "like his brethren in every respect, so that he might become a faithful high priest."

It is of a further stage in this "pioneering" in suffering that we read in I Peter 3: 19, that "he went and preached to the spirits in prison." The Gospels tell us of the interval between Jesus' death on the cross and His resurrection.

It is of this interval specifically that the Creed tells us, "He descended into hell." Cardinal Ratzinger wrote of this phrase, "If in the end one eliminates the statement altogether, one seems to have the advantage of getting rid of a curious idea, and one difficult to harmonize with our own modes of thought, without making oneself guilty of a particularly disloyal act" (**Introduction to Christianity**, p. 194). The future Pope Benedict XVI's comments in this part of the book offer penetrating insights on this article in the Apostles' Creed not present in other early creeds and impinging on sensibilities of the "God is dead" movement.

During this interval between Jesus death and resurrection hints are given us of what He did. Who these "spirits in prison" were, is left unexplained, but the very idea suggested by these two words is of the most profound suffering. When we recite the Creed and remember that, "He descended into hell," we speak of Jesus' going beyond the suffering of the cross in our behalf.

Most of you read our church newsletter this past week which included the moving letter Susan Cummings wrote to me about little David's death two years ago. Part of what touched me in this letter was the detail of David's suffering that she had to watch. As his mother, she no doubt felt more agony watching her little son suffer than if she had endured the suffering herself. Susan saw not only the cancer which invaded David's body, but she saw each pain-giving act of the very doctors and nurses who were trying to care for him.

She saw every bit of his suffering in this alien place, the hospital. The nurses and all those that cared for David were immensely compassionate. Yet Susan told us that she gained some intimations of how God must have felt in sending His Son to this alien place to suffer for us. His home was in heaven. David belonged at home, but he had to go there, to a place that was foreign and full of pain. Of course, David's reason for being sent to the hospital was different for our Lord's descent to be with us. David's was to find his own healing, our Lord's for our healing.

I could not help but notice, as I have thought about the section of the Apostles' Creed now before us, that in describing Jesus' death for us, we must be getting some glimpse of the detail God saw in watching His Son die for us. What happens in every pediatric hospital where little children sometimes suffer and die under the watchful eyes of their parents is an analogy of the heavenly Father's participation in Jesus' suffering for us. Jesus, God's beloved Son, belonged with His Father. But He came to this alien hospital to suffer at the hands of those He came to heal.

The suffering of Christ, we suppose, begins with the words "He suffered under Pontius Pilate." But doesn't it really begin with "He was conceived by the Holy Spirit, born of the Virgin Mary?" After all, this is where the Son of God "leaves home," and goes to the hospital to begin life with and for all of us who are ill.

Then, skipping over Jesus' life, we remember step by step His death's agonies:

"He suffered under Pontius Pilate"—how He suffered, with all the sleeplessness, insults, the thorny crown, and beatings, carrying a crude wooden cross on shoulders wounded by the lash of whips studded with hard bits intended to shred the flesh—before being crucified, a merciless way to die. We don't say all of that, of course, but we know this was how it was. Then He died, we say, and was buried. On the cross Jesus said, "It is finished," but there was more to come.

All the early forms of the Apostles' Creed stop at this point. Ignatius, in the second century, knew a Creed that said Jesus "also truly was raised from the dead," after declaring that He died on the cross. No mention of any descent into hell. Irenaeus sums up the whole painful death of Jesus by declaring: "He suffered under Pontius Pilate." That's all.

Some modern English renderings of this phrase exchange the word "the dead" for "hell." Indeed, it seems more than an odd place for the Son of God to go. So, let me make a brief diversion to notice some of the early fumblings with this term.

One fourth-century creed, the Fourth Formula of Sirmium, alluding to Job 38: 17, renders this phrase, "the Lord died and descended to the underworld and regulated things there, Whom the gate-keepers of hell saw and shuddered." Another fourth-century Church father, Rufinus, thought that when I Peter 3: 19 teaches that after death Christ "went and preached to the spirits in prison," it meant, to hell. In Latin the term is *descendit ad inferna*, the word from which we derive our conception of the hottest kind of fire, an inferno.

John Calvin calls our attention to the passages that tell us of Jesus' dread of death, which was a fear of far more than mere dying. Jesus prayed, "Father, save me from this hour" (John 12:27). On the cross He prayed, "My God, my God, why have you forsaken me," no longer calling God, "Father." It was not merely from death, physical death, that Jesus delivered us, but from sin, the cause of death, that He bore on His shoulders. His Father would not look at this. Paul wrote, "He became sin for us." Somehow, in dealing sin its death-blow, Jesus took on the full fury of God's wrath against sin. We cannot imagine how this was. The Creed declares, "He descended into hell," not meaning just the place of the dead, of which the psalmist wrote, "If I make my bead in hell, behold thou are there" (Psalm 139: 8).

Though we think of Jesus descent into hell, the accounts of Jesus' death in the Gospels tell us that Jesus said to one thief, "This day you will be with me in Paradise" (Luke 23: 43). How could Jesus descend into hell, if He was going directly to Paradise? It's a good question.

An answer may go something like this: God saw more happen after Jesus died than we can. St. Paul hints at this "more" in the passage from Ephesians I read for you moments ago: "He descended into the lower parts of the earth." We read the enigmatic words of I Peter 3:18-20, about His "being put to death in the flesh but made alive in the spirit; in which he went and preached to the spirits in prison." Did Jesus imply that this thief would pass quickly through the stages of the afterlife that we mean when we say "Hades," and then arrive with Jesus in Paradise? These passages of Scripture that relate to the afterlife are not presented in sequence with an explanation.

There are other New Testament passages that refer to fearful places that are **not** drawn into the discussion of where Jesus went during that period between His death on the cross and Easter morning.

Matthew 25 tells three parables, first of foolish virgins that come to a wedding feast only to be excluded because they didn't bring enough oil for their lamps until the bridegroom arrived. After this we read the parable which concludes with a lazy servant being consigned to "the outer darkness where men weep and gnash their teeth." Last, the parable of sheep and goats that ends with the goats that have been unresponsive to human need and therefore to Jesus' need, doomed to eternal punishment.

Jesus doesn't say that he joins any of these that are punished. Nor would that be pertinent because these are parables, stories not to be taken literally in their detail but, to be sure, seriously in their intent.

A fellow bishop asked the great Bishop Augustine of Hippo if Christ emptied hell when He descended to the place of the spirits in prison, freeing all the ones in it from Noah's day who perished in the flood, as Peter seems to suggest. St. Augustine wrote a lengthy letter back to him in which he began by saying, "I refer the question back to you, that if either you or any other person is able to do so, you may end my perplexities on the subject." If he was perplexed by this, perhaps we may be too.

St. Augustine observed that in Peter's great Pentecost sermon he quoted Psalm 16:10 as a prophecy of what would happen in the Messiah's life. The psalmist wrote, "Thou wilt not leave my soul in hell" (16: 10). Had Augustine known Hebrew it might have helped him. Some early Christian Bible teachers, untutored in Hebrew, thought Peter meant that Jesus, in effect, set up a little church in the place of the damned, where He preached successfully to those myriads of people who died up until the time of His death on the cross.

St. Augustine rejected this idea. He suggested that by "hell," perhaps was meant merely the future generations who would hear the Gospel preached but not respond with belief. Unbelieving people are "locked up in a prison of darkness." In their darkness they hear Jesus speak to them; they believe and are saved.

Perhaps this is as unconvincing to you as it is to me. But I have summarized many pages of St. Augustine's letter, which at no point really answers the question as we would like. If this was an insoluble problem for Augustine, perhaps we must acknowledge it is also for us.

When we turn to the Heidelberg Catechism which has instructed us so well on many questions, we find that it informs us that Jesus' descent into hell merely refers to Jesus' extreme distress and anguish that he suffered during the entire period of His passion. Ursinus who wrote this catechism, wrote in his commentary on Question 44, "Why is there added: 'He descended into hell?' That in my severest tribulations I may be assured that Christ my Lord has redeemed me from hellish anxieties and torment by the unspeakable anguish, pains, and terrors which he suffered in his soul both on the cross and before."

Augustine wrote on in the letter to which I have referred, "It was necessary for Christ to deliver us from the anguish and pains of hell. And this he did either before or after his death. It was not after his death. Therefore, it was before his death. Neither was it in his body that he endured these things; for the sufferings of his body were only external. Therefore, he suffered them in his soul." In other words, he tells us, the hell to which Jesus descended was on the cross itself, where He endured God's wrath against our sin.

So much has been written about this little sentence in the Creed, that in speaking to you about it I am tempted to make this merely a lesson in historical theology. Sometimes we can't help but be interested to know some of the process by which the Church has arrived at its teachings.

Perhaps we are to understand this phrase, "He descended into hell," as a statement of the extent of God's love for us.

People who love give and give. God, even more so. The God who loves us, gave and gave. He not only sent His Son on a Mission that required Him to "empty Himself, and take the form of a servant," which was extreme, but that required Him ultimately to do even more than this for us.

Paul closes the majestic "Christ hymn" in Philippians 2 with these words: "Therefore God has highly exalted him and give him a name which is above every name, that at the name of Jesus every knee shall bow, in heaven, on earth, and under the earth, and every tongue confess that Jesus Christ is Lord, to the glory of God the Father." Had the phrase "under the earth" not been there "the great majority" of those God created would be excluded. The reach of God's grace is displayed sweepingly in this closing doxology, where the Lordship of the One who gave Himself for us, spells out the full extent of the "us." Luke Timothy Johnson doesn't linger on this part of the Apostles' Creed because his book is on the Nicene Creed, but it is fitting to close remembering his remark, "The descent into hell . . . an expression of God's universal will for salvation and a part of the cosmic victory" (p. 175).

Let us pray: Lord God, we cannot understand what it means that Jesus descended into hell for us, but we understand enough to know that love for us could not have gone any farther. And for that we are grateful. In Jesus' name. Amen.

The Third Day He Rose Again from the Dead
Job 19:23-27; Mark 16:1-8

It is interesting that on a Sunday when we remember Jesus' resurrection that we should read from the Book of Job. The passage we read isn't really about a resurrection at all, but the Church has treated it as if it is. We do so because of a phrase in Job's reply to Bildad the Shuhite, who had accused Job in a final stinging word, "Such are the dwellings of the ungodly, such is the place of him who knows not God."

Job replies, "I know that my redeemer lives and at last he will stand upon the earth." It is the word "redeemer" (*goel* in Hebrew) that is our warrant for treating this as a passage from Job pertinent to Jesus' resurrection. In context Job is referring to the one that will vindicate him, that is, who will prove false all the criticism his accusers have imposed on top of his suffering. Yet, the word "redeemer" reminds us of Jesus, who has redeemed us from sin and death, as well as in reply to that would accuse us.

There are those that think that Jesus' resurrection was a thing of words and thoughts, an event that took place in the minds of His grieving followers. Consumed with love for Him, despairing His death, something of Him arose in their minds so forceful that they felt He lived in their heart. Though gone from them He now animated them with a power they had not experienced before. This was the "Easter Event" that was the substance of their "Easter Faith." This was the fount of that impulse that made Christians multiply in the next three hundred years so that Christianity became the dominant religion in the Roman Empire.

As I listened to this line of thought one Easter afternoon from a broadcast of an Easter sermon of a local congregation, I remembered John Updike's well-muscled words in his poem, "Seven Stanzas at Easter."

Make no mistake; if He rose at all
It was as His body;
If the cells' dissolution did not reverse,
the molecules
reknit, the amino acids rekindle;
the Church will fall.

It was not as the flowers,
Each soft Spring recurrent;
It was not as His Spirit in the mouths
And fuddled
Eyes of the eleven apostles;
Make no mistake; if He rose at all
it was as His flesh: ours.

The same hinged thumbs and toes,
the same valved heart
that—pierced—died, withered, paused, and then
regathered out of enduring Might
new strength to enclose.

Let us not mock God with metaphor,
analogy, sidestepping, transcendence;
making of the event a parable, a sign painted in the
faded credulity of earlier ages:
let us walk through the door.

The stone is rolled back, not papier-mâché,
not a stone in a story,
but the vast rock of materiality that in the slow
grinding of time will eclipse for each of us
the wide light of day.

And if we will have an angel at the tomb,
Make it a real angel,
Weighty with Max Planck's quanta, vivid
With hair,
Opaque in the dawn light, robed in real
Linen
Spun on a definite loom.

Let us not seek to make it less monstrous,
for our own convenience, our own sense of beauty,
lest, awakened in one unthinkable hour, we are
embarrassed by the miracle,
and crushed by remonstrance.

Jesus' resurrection ought not to be a point of pride for us, as though this proves the superiority of Christianity. After all, the resurrection followed a death that we made needful for a God of love, who did not abandon us. Though we celebrate Easter in our churches with a brass ensemble adding brilliance to our hymns of triumph, it was God's act and not of our deserving.

Jesus' resurrection from death resonated with an intuition of other ancient peoples. The Egyptians' religion was fastened to a conviction that the dead would rise. They made mummies of their dead, so their bodies were prepared for resumption of life in the flesh.

The ancient Persians also had well-developed beliefs about the resurrection for good people after ordinary life (See A.V. Williams Jackson, "The Ancient Persian Doctrine of a Future Life," ***The Biblical World***, Vol. 8, No. 2 (Aug. 1896), pp. 149-163).

I do not put Judaism on a par with the religion of ancient Egypt, but in this regard, they were similar. The *Amidah*, a prayer Rabbi Sir Jonathan Sacks refers to as "the summit of prayer . . . in [which] we enter the holy of holies of religious experience," soon after blessing God, continues: "You are eternally mighty, Lord. You give life to the dead . . . who with great compassion revives the dead . . . and keeps faith with those who sleep in the dust . . . Faithful are You to revive the dead. Blessed are you, Lord, who revives the dead." (***The Koren Siddur***, Jerusalem, 2009, p. 110).

Rabbi Pinchas Lapide, wrote in his little book, ***The Resurrection of Jesus; a Jewish Perspective*** (1982), "Perhaps the most Jewish characteristic of the Nazarene is his immortal, powerful hope which found its pinnacle, beyond cross and tomb, in the faith of his resurrection—a faith which, in the unsearchable ways of God for salvation, led to the birth of Christianity" (p. 30).

The poem Updike wrote was not an extreme statement. Instead, it is a corrective to the smothering of the Gospels' teaching that has been reduced to a "doctrine" of the second chance. You may have experienced failure, this erosion of the Gospel's message explains, give it another try. "If at first you don't succeed, try and try again." You can, as it were, rise from the dead.

Those that joined the small company of Christians in the early days and years, were not lured to Jesus by any notions of a second chance in life. Theirs was a robust confidence that Jesus' body rose from death, and, as Paul put it, "the first fruits of them that sleep" (I Corinthians 15: 20). The entire chapter in which Paul wrote that memorable phrase explains why Jesus' resurrection from death mattered to thousands of people so that the population of the early Church exploded. Then, trusting in God's triumph over death in Jesus' resurrection "devoted themselves to the apostles' teaching, and fellowship, to the breaking of bread, and the prayers." It was a new way of life anchored in a settled conviction that Jesus was "risen indeed."

Looking back today we marvel at the explosion of the early Church from its tiny beginning in Jerusalem so that within 40 years it had penetrated the Mediterranean world and beyond. The Church was planted westward in Britain and as far East as India before jet airplanes had shrunk the world to the small size of our day.

Unlike the conquests of Islam in the 7th and 8th centuries, which changed all North Africa from Christianity to Islam, and very nearly did the same thing to Europe, no swords were part of the advance of earliest Christianity. The Christians' armor was that described by Paul in Ephesians, "the whole armor of God . . . the breastplate of righteousness;" their shoes the "gospel of peace." It was this armament that conquered the hearts of many people that were convinced that Jesus had done what no other man ever did, escaped a tomb alive—for a purpose. His resurrection did not prove that He was the Son of God, but it convinced many that what He taught and did corresponded fully with His rising from death to life. We refer to "doubting Thomas" with a chipper kind of disdain, but none of Jesus' disciples believed at first. They didn't exactly charge to the tomb on Easter morning to cheer Jesus' triumph over death. The women came to the tomb had to persuade them.

But once Jesus' first followers were convinced, they became a vibrant society that multiplied exponentially.

In the early 4th century Licinius, the Emperor in the Western part of the Roman Empire, tried to purge all Christians from his army. One story stands out in illustration of how the sword in the hands of the enemies, instead of suppressing this faith, helped it to spread.

Licinius commanded all Christians among his soldiers to identify themselves. In one of his legions, "The Thundering Legion," situated at Sebaste (Samaria), the commanding officer ordered the 40 soldiers who confessed their faith in Jesus to take off their clothes and walk out on a frozen lake. To make the temptation to renounce Christ more appealing he had fires built along the shore. The 40 men sang of their commitment to Jesus as they stood freezing to death on the ice. From time to time one of these tormented Christian soldiers lost heart and returned to the shore when the appeal of the warming fires grew strong. But, we're told, for each soldier who could not endure, another of Licinius' soldiers would step into his place. Forty Christian soldiers froze to death rather than renounce Jesus.

Their courage came to be widely known and drew many people to trust in this Jesus. The bond that drew Christians together was very cordial.

It was said of the early Christians, "How they love one another." This is not always the case simply for "very religious" people. It was said of them, 'My how they love one another."

So, I want to say to you who are joining our congregation this morning, not only trust in Jesus' resurrection, but also let it be said of you, "How they love one another."

Our devotion to the risen Christ is to be evident in our devotion to each other. What ultimately binds us to Jesus and to each other? We might say, it is the resurrection of Jesus from the grave.

But we cannot disconnect the resurrection of Jesus from the love that compelled Jesus to die for us. The resurrection is God's gift guaranteeing that life for us does not end when our hearts stop beating. But Jesus' death is the metaphor of the Christian life. Paul wrote in his Epistle that is described as the "charter of Christian liberty, words that might seem odd for such a writing: "I am crucified with Christ, nevertheless I live. And the life that I now live in the flesh I live by the faith of the Son of God who gave His life for me" (Galatians 2: 20). Jesus' resurrection, then, is the capstone of Jesus' passion, demonstrating that His death was not in vain.

Let these truths bind us to Jesus and to one another.

Let us pray: Lord God, thank you for Jesus: for His life, for His death for us, and for His resurrection. Grant us the devotion, in our distracted age, to do these things, that flesh out our gratitude. For Jesus' sake. Amen.

Jesus Ascended into Heaven
Isaiah 6:1-5; Acts 1:1-11

Two weeks ago, on this day, though a bit earlier in the day, I stood with two dear friends around the altar at St. Gregory's Abbey chapel, taking the Eucharist, or the Lord's Supper, as Protestant's say. But it seems a bit odd to say "Lord's Supper" of a sacred meal taken before dawn.

A few times in my life I've had the extraordinary sense of being in the presence of God, in a way I did not want to end. This was one of those times. In a remote way it seemed like what Isaiah describes in the passage we just read. Then, but not now, six-winged angels flew back and forth enthusiastically calling back and forth to each other, "Holy, Holy, Holy is the Lord of hosts!" I experienced different impressions of sense.

We had just heard the monks' subdued chanting of various psalms and then we sang together *a Capella* the hymn, "Once in David's Royal City."

The way a hymn echoes in that acoustically charmed wooden chapel lends a rare beauty to the singing. The words of Father William, who preached on the text, "The Word was made flesh and dwelt among us," had touched me deeply.

I go to the monastery at the end of each year to be lifted out of my usual surroundings, at least for a few days, to find a place in which holiness is nurtured at the start of the new year. There the busy world is hushed and pushed away, and prayer is unabashedly the main work of everyone. The monks come to pray the way you report to your office on a weekday morning.

Well, on that Sunday morning, two weeks ago, I sensed holiness invading my space. I saw Jesus and the sight was too beautiful for me to remain unmoved. Sometimes beautiful music will move us. As the warden puts it in Trollope's novel, "no music, no mystery." Now it was the beauty of holiness that moved me. With the smell of incense consecrating the air, filling the space above us with gentle swirls, we took the Lord's Supper. I heard in a fresh way Jesus' words, "This is my Body, broken for you." I wanted that moment to linger. We Protestant's don't take those words as literally as we should. How we "take" words matters in what they mean to us.

The moment didn't linger, but I've thought often since then that God does not give us these moments to waste on mere exquisite feelings at the time. God gives us special moments with Him to awaken us and to equip us for what He has for us to do and be in the time ahead. I wondered what that would be at Faith Church in 1994.

You're maybe thinking that I've dived a bit deeply into Anglo-Catholicism—bells and smells and all of that. Indeed, there are "bells and smells" aplenty at the Abbey church, and I enjoy all of that, at least there. I'm not sure you'd like me to bring this back here. Perhaps you'll allow us who went there the freedom to be touched by God in a setting different from what we're used to here.

Isaiah seems to have had a moment like the one I've described, only on a more super-charged scale. He was in the Temple doing His priestly service when he saw the Lord sitting on His throne. The wafting incense he saw was transformed in his mind's eye, becoming the train of God's royal robes who sat there.

Incense had a two-fold significance: it stood for prayer that ascends to God from His Temple; it also stood for the clouds that gather high above the earth, a nimbus engulfing God. Now it seemed the incense was something different from either clouds or prayers; God seemed visibly present.

The sight and the sounds overwhelmed him, and he said what anyone must say who encounters God so directly, "Woe is me; I am lost!" He was entirely out of his element.

But God gave Isaiah this vision for a reason. He had something for Isaiah to do. After this Isaiah heard God ask, "Whom shall I send, and who will go for us?" And Isaiah replied, "Here am I, send me."

A reflex thought hit me, that this anticipated the moment Jesus was in the home of Mary and Martha in Bethany, that had an opposite conclusion. For Isaiah God intended his moment alone to result in doing something. After Martha chided Mary for not getting busy Jesus defended Mary's adoration. The voice Isaiah heard spoke opposite to the voice Martha heard.

Of course, both kinds of response have their place. Mary once knelt before Jesus washing His feet. Was she the same unidentified woman that washed Jesus' feet with her tears of whom Luke wrote (Luke 7: 37 f), or the woman of whom Matthew's Gospel tells when Jesus was in another home in Bethany, Mary and Martha's home town. There another unidentified woman poured expensive ointment on Jesus feet. Matthew tells us Jesus said then, "Wherever this gospel is preached in the whole world, what she has done will be told in memory of her" (Matthew 26: 13).

I think the Lord would have us busy, doctrinally super-careful Protestants remember that there is a place for quiet adoration. No words just focus.

But for Isaiah at this mysterious moment, the purpose was to remind Isaiah of a task God had for him to do.

What if we were to find ourselves in rapt contemplation of our Lord today, and then come away wondering, "Why did this come to me"? I have read of others in the story of Christianity who "saw" God in mysterious ways. Some of these we celebrate if the person is famous.

Many that have never had a mystical experience of God remember these words of Pascal as mystical "proof" of the possibility of feeling what no argument can prove. What Pascal experienced was like the Apostle Paul's, in a way, that he described in II Corinthians 12. It was so vivid. It probably was a vision that God provided him to confirm the summons on his life that God first made as Saul was on the Damascus Road, bent on persecuting Christians. Of it Paul wrote, "I know a man in Christ, who fourteen years ago was caught up to the third heaven . . . I know that this man was caught up into Paradise."

For Paul as for Isaiah, this rare vision of God that induced intense adoration, had a purpose beyond the ecstatic moment. God had work for them to do.

We read of these experiences of God and maybe wish we had them too. But I would guess the three reports of women's adoringly washing Jesus' feet, or of Isaiah's and Paul's overwhelming mystical experiences are not given often so that we treat them as common. If we could know what the women did the rest of their lives after their intense moments with Jesus, perhaps we could see that for them too, the result was their lives' devotion to serving this Jesus they adored.

For them it became as the Son of Man spoke in the Matthew's account of the parable of the sheep and goats, that when they saw people in need, they saw Jesus in need, and served Him in serving them (Matthew 25: 31-46)

Everyone loves an inspiring worship service that moves us inwardly. But God gives us these inward moments to move us to do something. We need to respond, "Here am I." We suffer from feelings of purposelessness if our "mountain top experiences" do not have service as their sequel.

I'm not an enthusiast of tattoos as an art form, but I once had a very devout young woman study Hebrew with me who had the Hebrew words tattooed on one of her ankles, "hinenni," which means, "Here I am." Abraham replied these words when God addressed him by name, not knowing the awful task God had in store for him (Genesis 22: 1). Moses said this when God spoke to him out of the burning bush. Isaiah said this too in the passage we have read today. My student wanted to place herself in the queue with Abraham, Moses and Isaiah. "Here I am" too.

Our New Testament lesson shows us another such moment many years later for the disciples of Jesus. Forty days after rising from the grave, Jesus had His disciples about Him. He had something for them to do too. He was going to equip them by giving them an experience of Himself they would not forget.

Acts 1: 12 tells us this took place on Mt. Olivet. There is a Chapel of the Ascension at this place today. This moment marks the end of Jesus' immediate project begun in Bethlehem's stable.

Luke began to describe Jesus' path to His suffering and death with the words. "When the days drew near for him to be received up" (Luke 9:51). Neither Matthew nor Mark explicitly mention Jesus' ascension into heaven, but both tell us about the end of time when Jesus will come "with the clouds of heaven" (Matt. 16:27; 24:30; Mark 8:38;13:26).

The Apostle Paul reminded the Christians at Ephesus that the Jesus who came down to the depths of earth was the one who "ascended far above all the heavens" (Eph. 4:10). Mention of other events in Jesus' life are scarce as hen's teeth in Paul's writing. Why does Paul write to Jesus' ascension?

Perhaps it is because he heard from his travel companion, Luke, that he'd written the story of Jesus' life already. It was Paul's task to tell the purpose of Jesus' life, to die, to rise from death, and then to leave. So as Paul had written of Jesus' cross and resurrection, the briefly remembers Jesus' final moment on this planet.

Let's look again now of Jesus' ascension. At first as the disciples stood with Jesus the moment was "heavy" with anticipation; but anticipation of what? Did the disciples think they would finally see a display of preternatural power? Jesus was about to inaugurate His Kingdom for real—with power that would dwarf the power of the Roman legions?

Jesus had shown Himself stronger than the fury of the religious authorities who feared Him and stronger than the power of the Romans who crucified Him. He had come out of the sealed tomb more easily than a person gets out of bed in the morning. But instead of a new display of power in which Jesus unfurled His full messianic muscle, now they saw the opposite. Jesus gently lifted-off the earth, as we'd say of a NASA spacecraft headed for the moon. Jesus disappeared into the clouds.

We who know we don't live on a three-tiered universe read this and wonder what it means. So, what happened, really? If the most ardent skeptic would see this happen today, not in a Spielberg movie, where visual effects routinely happen, but before their very eyes, then what? You reply, it could not happen. It defies all we know about the universe and our tiny (immense) solar system. Besides, God is not into magic tricks. No magician's disappearing act here.

Luke says the disciples stood gazing upwards. We can visualize that. No doubt their jaws dropped, their mouths agape.

Two men that we take to be angels, stood by them, explaining what would come next. The disciples probably thought maybe Jesus' return would come later in the day. But that was not to be. They didn't recognize the two men that they suddenly saw with them. But of course, they'd not seen them before. Had they been first to the empty tomb on Easter morning, they might have recognized the two men that Luke described at the resurrection scene. Then they stood by Mary Magdalene, Joanna, and Mary "in dazzling apparel." (Luke 24: 4). Now it was with Jesus' disciples that these two men stood. We must imagine that there was a moment in which they were incredulous. Who are you to tell us anything? But the moment was "heavy," and this mysterious weight, this unexpected gravity opened them to believe what they heard. They were reassured. The promise of Jesus' return fortified them.

They went back to Jerusalem to the upper room where they had taken their last meal with Jesus.

For at least three of the disciples— Peter, James and John, this moment was reminiscent of another time when they had been with Jesus as He prayed, maybe on this same place. None of the Gospels tell us on what mountain they saw Jesus transfigured, but imagine it was this one. They recognized that earlier "heavy moment" when they saw Jesus with two men they recognized as Moses and Elijah. Now it was two different men they did not recognize that were with them. After Peter, James and John had come down from the mountain where Jesus was transfigured, they saw how helpless their fellow disciples were as they tried to help a demon-possessed boy.

Would they now leave this moment with Jesus only to be confronted with their own feebleness again?

But we know what happened, because we have just read the account. They had heard Jesus tell them, "You shall receive power when the Holy Spirit has come upon you; and you shall be my witnesses in Jerusalem. and in all Judea and Samaria, and to the end of the earth." The spectacular experience of seeing Jesus' ascension enforced in their minds that the One who had said "you will be My witnesses" was the very One who had been "in the beginning with God," and who was now returning to Him. Yet, he promised "I will be with you."

This was no mere suggestion from a friend going on a journey. Jesus' concluding command to His followers was the culmination of His entire work with them. Now the reason for it all was clear, He had come to do the will of the Father to commission them to continue to do the work of the Father.

Now the disciples were in a "Here am I, send me" moment. We still enjoy the benefits of what they did.

I would like to encourage you here this morning to remember this story that is our story too.

I hope that we may catch a glimpse of the Holiness of God in His temple that awakened Isaiah to receive the task he was to do, and of the ascension of Jesus to His Father's right hand that impelled the earliest disciples of Jesus to penetrate their world with the Gospel within their generation. The same voice says to us: "You will be my witnesses in Jerusalem, and in all Judea, and in Samaria, and to the ends of the earth."

I hope that the time we spend in this place may provide for us a glimpse of Jesus that will thrill others that have not seen Jesus

We don't know when Jesus will come again. No one knows, so it must not matter when. In the meantime, He sends us into the world so that his work may become our work, even when we are "at work." To do our work as unto Him; to be husbands and wives, friends and fellow workers, as unto Him; we continue the work Jesus gave His disciples to do.

Let us pray: We praise you, O God; we acknowledge You to be the Lord. All the earth worships You, the Father everlasting. To You all angels cry aloud: the heavens, and all the powers in it. To You cherubim and seraphim continually do cry— "Holy, Holy, Holy Lord God of Sabaoth." Heaven and earth are full of the majesty, of your glory. The glorious company of the apostles praise you. The goodly fellowship of the prophets praises You. The noble army of martyrs praise You. The holy Church throughout the world acknowledge You to be the Father of infinite majesty, and your only Son, Jesus, and the Holy Spirit. O Lord God, we here acknowledge You to be our Lord. We offer You ourselves and say, "Here am I, send me." Amen.

Jesus Sits at the Right Hand of God, the Father
Psalm 110; Mark 16:9-20

Our Gospel lesson this morning is from a disputed passage in the Gospel of Mark. It is a passage that some devout Christians in our country believe means they should demonstrate their faith by handling poisonous snakes without being bit.

Verses 9-20 of Mark's last chapter are missing from some early manuscripts; but are present in some. It has been read by Christians since the early days of the Church. The reason why every undisputed part of the New Testament possesses its canonical status is this "silent" witness to its inspiration: it is widely accepted in the Church. The formula of Vincent of Lerins after the third ecumenical Council of Ephesus (AD 431), that the standard for the acceptance of a doctrine was that it is accepted "always by all, everywhere, by everyone" (*quod semper quod ubique quod ab omnibus*) was never achieved. Nearly everyone was as good as possible. Thus, was demonstrated by widespread adherence and the pronouncement of a Church council what was the true teaching of the Church. Well, this longer ending of Mark's Gospel has enjoyed widespread use and is challenged only on the basis of less than complete attestation in all manuscripts.

And for sure it includes more specifically than anywhere else the phrase in the Creed that the risen Christ is "seated at the right hand of the Father."

That this passage also includes this teaching about handling poisonous serpents safely perhaps refers to the Apostle Paul's experience after surviving a shipwreck off the coast of Malta. While picking up some sticks to build a fire, a viper latched onto his hand. Vipers are deadly as you know. People assumed it was God's judgment on Paul, a criminal on his say to trial, but he was none the worse for wear. God protected him. As a result, people changed their tune from thinking he was a criminal to thinking him a god (Acts 28: 1-6).

Here may be a good place to say that one of the delights of the Bible is interruptions in it to our figuring everything out. When we come on to them we should chuckle at ourselves, remembering what Paul told us that "if we have all knowledge. I am nothing." Let's respect our snake-handling brothers and sisters, whose trust in God's protection is so complete that they take Mark 16: 18 as a promise to fortify their faith. I'll not be joining them any time soon, but maybe if I did I'd discover that they are doing better at exhibiting marks of a Christian that I feel sure are not in question.

Well, Jesus sitting on the right hand of the Father, as Mark 16: 19 tells us, came to be recited as a building block of our faith. After Jesus ascended into heaven he "sat down at the right hand of God."

We are not to imagine a heavenly scene of the Holy Trinity now sitting back, as it were, in a celestial hall that makes Westminster Abbey look like a slum, basking in the "finished work of Christ." Indeed, Jesus told His disciples, "I will be with you to the close of the age" (Matthew 38: 19). Or as we read in Hebrews 13: 5, "I will never fail you nor forsake you." Earlier in this same NT book we read, "he always lives to make intercession for [us]" (7: 25). Clearly there is a difference between the picture of Jesus sitting at the right hand of the father, praying for us, and being with us wherever we are, praying for us continually.

This is a phrase in the Creed that not only reminds us of the unity of purpose of the first and second persons of the Holy Trinity, but also tells us to remember that Jesus is not only our Savior, indeed, our Lord, but also our untiring cheer leader. As Paul wrote about God's place in this suffering world, "Such a mixture of pictures of Jesus after His suffering and death that we have!

Furthermore, we notice that here is not a complete display of our conception of God as triune; three Persons, but one God. This comes in the third section of the Creed.

But let us accept how we should think of Jesus as the Creed explains to this point.

One of the most obvious features of a successful basketball season at Purdue is that up in the stands the players know they've got an awful lot of people cheering them on; 14,123 of them, to be exact, we're told. They flock to Mackey Arena well in advance of every game.

But we sports fans are a fickle lot. When our teams are down, and need the most encouragement, they are apt to see less fan support and to "hear" silence during the game; perhaps boos instead of cheers. For the past four years our young football players needed cheering to perk them up because they weren't winning. They were discouraged because they were losing; they were losing because they were playing discouraged. But when they needed encouragement the most they got the least.

From the tone of voice of our local radio sports announcers, to the editorial writers of the local paper, to the remarks of folk waiting in line to check out at the grocery store, the evidence mounts that we encourage our winners, not our losers. Sometimes people can get down-right mean at the time our youngsters are the most vulnerable.

I think of this in keeping with what the Creed reminds us about Jesus His ascension. He sat at the right-hand side of God the Father. We may ask, "Doing what?" "He ever lives to make intercession for us." (Hebrews 7: 25).

One of my favorite hymns, composed by the eighteenth century Moravian pastor, Nicholas von Zinzendorf has a line that puts together Jesus' death for us and His on-going care for us. "I trust the ever-living One, His wounds for me shall plead." It's a turn of phrase that is maybe a bit unseemly, but its sense of the benefit of the Cross is vivid. How can we know God will always care for us? Because of what it cost Him to offer this care.

Paul asked the rhetorical question, "If God is for us, who can be against us? He who did not spare his own son, how shall he not, with him, freely give us everything else?" Indeed, as Paul goes on to write, "nothing can separate us from the love of God in Christ our Lord."

The most optimistic words in the Bible are found in this section. There the Apostle Paul exclaims as much as asks: "If God is for us, who can be against us?" Here he lists many of life's most severe tests: "tribulation, distress, persecution, famine, nakedness, peril, the sword." Fill in your own tests: temptation to despair, trying situations at work, heart aches within your family, sickness, feelings of having little worth.

What we call "sin" is sometimes misinterpreted. We don't distinguish too well between what God probably considers sin and what our society tells us is sin. Paul tells us in another place, that there is no trial of any kind that we face that is not faced by everyone else (I Corinthians 10: 13).

But that's another point to ponder. But here I would hope we see that in all these difficulties where we feel like losers, we are winners. Winners? Yes, winners! Why? Because God is for us! When all is said and done, this is what matters. God is for us.

In a nutshell, this is the assuring truth that we remind ourselves of each time we say the little phrase in the Apostles' Creed, "Jesus sits at the right hand of God, the Father Almighty." The very picture of Christ sitting rather than pacing back and forth is reassuring.

When the Bible gives us this picture of Jesus sitting at the right hand of the Father, we are only to try to understand what the right-hand side stands for. We are, in a sense, to picture a heavenly throne room, with God seated on the throne, and Jesus sitting at His right hand. But when I say, "in a sense," we must realize that it is just this, and no more than this. This is one of those teachings in the Bible where an earthly analogy is offered to us as an illustration of a deep truth, even though its physical description has no counterpart in heaven.

In the 110th Psalm, a Messianic psalm, David wrote: "The Lord says to my Lord, 'Sit at my right hand, till I make your enemies your footstool.'"

It is a scene that the Old Testament sets for us, and which the Scriptures remind us that Jesus, after ascending after His resurrection, was seated at God's right hand (Mark 16:19; Acts 5:31; Romans 8:34; Ephesians 1:20).

There is another aspect to this picture of Jesus. As Paul put it in Philippians 2 His ascension to the Father's right hand puts him a royal pose. But it is a gracious royalty we see. "At the name of Jesus every knee will bow, of things in heaven, on the earth, and under the earth, and every tongue confess, that Jesus Christ is Lord, to the glory of God the Father." I sense that all who bow are united in realizing, with gratitude what this seated Monarch of the universe did for them. It will be a privilege to bow there.

When He came here, "He emptied Himself" of so many of the prerogatives of Deity that "He was despised and rejected by men." He became, in fact, "a man of sorrows," as Isaiah put it.

But time moves on, and Jesus Christ's full character comes on display. Paul asks, "Who is to condemn us? Is it Christ who died, yes, who was raised from the dead, who is at the right hand of God, who indeed intercedes for us?" It is a rhetorical question to which the answer is a resounding NO! Jesus does not condemn us. After all, when God was nearest to us, seeing all the foibles and weaknesses of humans up close and personal, feeling the cruelty of humanity's most pitiless soldiers, rather than being filled with a desire for revenge, He was filled with compassion and forgiveness instead.

Jesus always has been FOR us.

In our more reflective, introspective moments we see much of the evidence in ourselves that God might use to reject us: we are not very forgiving of people who do the very things we do; we find it easier to turn our eyes away when we see people in need, whom we could help, than to inconvenience ourselves for their sake; we don't love our neighbors as we love ourselves— the standard we hold for caring for others is not the standard we hold for our own wellbeing. To put it generously, we are apt to play a bit loose with the truth when we think it is to our advantage; we have a "convenience test" in keeping our promises.

This is a partial list, we all know. Our memories are like tape recorders catching all the evidence needed to convict us of our sin. Jesus saw all of this "up close and personal" during His time on earth.

The natural reflex in people is to think of God, then, as a Judge who is weighing our good deeds against our bad deeds. People who think of God this way then try to fool themselves into thinking their good deeds outweigh their bad deeds. But this is a sorry line of reasoning to take.

The remarkable message of the Gospel is that the One who is now "seated at the right hand of the Father" is not our judge but our advocate. John tells us, "If anyone sin, we have an advocate with the Father, Jesus Christ the righteous One" (I John 2:1). Paul tells us that Jesus intercedes for us (Romans 8:34).

The overwhelming picture we get from the passages of the Bible I have drawn together, is that the One who knows our every weakness is a continual "mediator" in our behalf before God (I Timothy 2:5).

We are going to repeat together, in a minute or so, the answer to question 49 of the Heidelberg catechism. I will ask you, "What benefit do we receive from Christ's ascension into heaven?" And you will say there are three benefits: first, that Jesus is our Advocate before the Father, second, that Jesus, in His presence there, is anticipating our presence there, and third, that He has sent the Holy Spirit to work for good in us. And so, it is.

Before I close, I want to take this truth and suggest one way we should apply this in our own experience. If Jesus pleads in your behalf, even though you fail, should you and I not be for one another too, particularly when we fail?!

Let us pray: Gladly, Lord God, we claim the promise, "If God is for us, who can be against us. Grant us to understand how to live hearing the sound that comes at your right hand, where He who is for us, speaks in our behalf. Amen

From There He Will Come to Judge of the Living and the Dead
I Chronicles 16:28-36; II Timothy 4:1-8

Today is a very special day at Faith Church because I will baptize a family into the Church. We will do what seems to be described twice in Acts 16. Someone who has come to believe in Jesus is baptized "and all his house." Evan Janovitz will be baptized along with his and Patti's children, Nathan, Jason, Francis and Oliver. Patti was baptized as a child. It is a great joy to me to administer this Sacrament to members of a family that has become very dear to us over the past months.

In the providence of God, the topic of my sermon today is the phrase from the Apostles' Creed, "From thence He shall come to judge the living and the dead." You might think this an odd topic for a sermon on a day when we welcome a family into the Church. But this phrase comes next in our progress through the Apostles' Creed.

It is nearly a universal view that after people die they must answer for how they have lived. One of the most interesting examples of this comes from ancient Egypt, a nation saturated with religion. There developed **The Egyptian Book of the Dead** from coffin texts that early pharaohs had chiseled into the walls of their mausoleums, the pyramids. The copy in the British Museum is made of thirty-seven papyrus sheets stitched together. It is seventy-eight feet long. At first the coffin texts were a guide through the after-life for kings. It evolved into general use. The center piece of this elaborately illustrated document tells of a "Weighing of the Heart" ceremony that everyone faces after they die.

The one that has died is led before Osiris, the deity presiding over the under-world. Forty-three other deities surround the judgment hall. Before this awesome assembly the dead person must give a negative confession, naming the offenses of which he/she is not guilty. "I have never stolen. I have never knowingly told lies. I did not diminish the offerings in the temple. I did not destroy things that were made, etc."

The dead person's heart which has been removed from the body is put on one side of a balance scale as Thoth, the scribe of the gods looks on. The other side of the scale has on it a feather of Maat, the goddess of truth, order, and justice. If the heart being weighed is heavier than the feather of Maat, the person was delivered over to Ammit, a ferocious creature part crocodile, with the front legs of a lion and the back legs of a hippopotamus that will deliver the person to oblivion. If the person's heart was as light as the feather of Maat, the deceased is granted a place in the fields of Hetep and Iaru, a place of delight, to await the sure and certain resurrection to come.

What has been delivered to us about the after-life is not so picturesque as the Egyptian idea. The Apostles' Creed only tells us that after Jesus ascended to heaven, "from thence He will come to judge the living and the dead."

The Bible has much to say about the judgment, but this aspect of the Bible's teaching is not much spoken of today. Hebrews 9: 27 states laconically, "It is appointed unto men to die once, and after this comes the judgement." But it goes on, "so Christ . . . will appear a second time to save those who are eagerly waiting for him." The verse following the oft-quoted John 3: 16 states: "For God sent the Son into the world, not to condemn the world, but that the world might be saved through him."

In the Bible there is a tension between God's salvation and the judgment of God. Jesus did not come to condemn the world because the world already stood under the judgment of God.

Why the great flood described in detail in Genesis? Because "the Lord saw that the wickedness of man was great in the earth . . . And the Lord was sorry that he had made man on the earth" (Genesis 6: 5-6). Why the Tower of Babel incident after which human language was scrambled? Because humanity had become arrogant, planning to build a tower that would reach the domain of God, heaven (Genesis 11: 4).

Why was Israel, God's chosen people, taken into exile from the Promised Land that "flowed with milk and honey?" Deuteronomy 28: 15 told why. "If you will not obey the voice of the Lord your

God or be careful to do all his commandments . . . then all these curses shall overtake you." The curses included being conquered by "a nation that neither you nor your fathers have known, and there you shall serve other gods, of wood and stone. And you shall become a horror, a proverb, and a byword, among all the peoples where the Lord your God will lead you away" (28: 36-37).

The theme of God's judgment then came to have a prominent place in their sacred Scriptures.

Listen to some of this litany of judgment: Psalm 9:7, "The Lord shall endure forever: he has prepared his throne for judgment." and Ecclesiastes 12:13-14, "Fear God and keep his commandments: for this is the whole duty of man. For God will bring every deed into judgment, with every secret thing, whether good or evil." Jeremiah wrote for God: "I, the Lord, search the heart, I try the reins [i.e., kidneys, the deepest part], even to give every man according to his ways, and according to the fruit of his doings" (17:10). The prophet Amos said, "Prepare to meet thy God, O Israel."

The one that translated the psalms into Greek for the Jewish people in exile in Egypt, that no longer knew Hebrew, changed the fearful words of Psalm 7: 12, "God is angry with the wicked every day" to "God is a righteous judge . . . not bringing forth his anger every day."

I wonder if this in the Greek translation of the psalms underlies Paul's statement, "Where sin abounded grace did much more abound" (Romans 5: 20). Indeed, God's grace, His unearned favor is a strong theme in the New Testament. But God's judgment is still there. And the judgment is worse because it involves consequences in the afterlife.

Jesus taught us, "I tell you, on the day of judgment men will render account for every careless word they utter" (Matt. 12:36). Again, he said: "The Son of man shall come in the glory of his Father with his angels; and then he shall reward every man according to his works" (Matt. 16:27).

Jesus' parables of judgment in Matthew 25 are so severe that they can produce night-mares. I hear one small snippet of this chapter quoted often, the part that reminds us of the importance of feeding the hungry, and clothing the naked, visiting the imprisoned, and giving water to the thirsty. But rarely is what comes next mentioned, the consequences of not offering this care. Those that do not feed the hungry, cloth the naked, and visit the imprisoned, Jesus said will be "cast into outer darkness where there is weeping and gnashing of teeth."

The New Testament teaches us specific things about this judgment to come. It is on this teaching that the writers of the Apostles' Creed base the statement. "From thence he (Jesus) shall come to judge both the quick and the dead." Jesus will do the judging, and the dead will be raised to get their turn before this tribunal.

To the rich and powerful that lived in the splendid comfort of the resort city, Caesarea by the sea, Peter said, "God commanded us to testify that he [Jesus] is the one ordained by God to be judge of the living and the dead" (Acts 10:42). "He will," Paul wrote, "bring to light the hidden things of darkness and will disclose the purposes of the heart" (I Corinthians 4:5).

Indeed, one of the clearest teachings of the Old and New Testament is that we are accountable for how we live. Perhaps the most sobering statement Jesus made. that challenges the very relaxed ideas of what it is to be a Christian that are taught (or thought) today is found in Matthew 7:21-23, "Not everyone who says to me 'Lord. Lord.' shall enter the kingdom of heaven. but he who does the will of my Father who is in heaven. On that day many will say to me. 'Lord, Lord, did we not prophesy in your name and cast out demons in your name and do many mighty works in your name?' And then will I declare to them. "I never knew you, depart from me, you evildoers."

What to do with all this that is so different from "Amazing grace, how sweet the sound that saved a wretch like me?" We are more comfortable emphasizing Paul's teaching about the grace of God, and that salvation comes to us by faith alone. Indeed, since the Protestant Reformation great emphasis has been put on God's freely given grace and that we cannot earn our salvation, that some might think Paul frowns on good behavior. To emphasize goodness seems to diminish the need for God's grace.

I wonder if the Church does well in portraying Jesus from only one side as Savior, ignoring what the Bible tells us of Jesus as judge.

From some in my trade I get the impression that pleasing God has become a matter of showing up in full-dress human weakness.

What has become of "Pass the time of your sojourning here in fear" (I Peter 1:17). Again, he writes: "If after (you) have escaped the pollutions of the world through the knowledge of the Lord and Savior Jesus Christ, (you) are again entangled therein, and overcome, the latter end is worse than the beginning. It had been better not to have known the way of righteousness than after having known it to turn from the holy commandment delivered to (you)" (II Peter 2:20).

Hebrews tells us soberly, "If we sin willfully after we have received the knowledge of the truth, there remains no more sacrifice for sins" (Hebrews 10:26).

The Apostle Paul, who taught us of "grace alone," agonized personally that after he had preached the Gospel to others, he should be a castaway (I Corinthians 9: 27).

I would be derelict in my duty to you not to remind you that these all are part of the teaching of Scripture. Popular Christendom has cheerfully carved for itself a "canon within the canon," a selection of fortunate quotations that can be tucked into a comforting system of right and proper belief alone.

It has not always been this way. Many years ago, in our land there was an earth-shaking movement called by historians, "The Great Awakening." This movement in the first half of the 18th century produced some widely publicized sermons and stories of conversions. Jonathan Edwards' sermon at Enfield, Connecticut in 1741, "Sinners in the hands of an angry God" is probably the best-known sermon of this period. His text was Deut. 32:35, "Their foot shall slide in due time."

Not a few people since have referred to this sermon with nervous amusement. You've maybe heard those celebrated lines: "The God that holds you over the pit of Hell much as one holds a spider or some loathsome insect over the fire abhors you and is dreadfully provoked. . . Consider the fearful danger you are in." He ended this sermon with the lines from Genesis 19:17, "Escape for thy life; look not behind thee ... escape to the mountain, lest thou be consumed."

Everyone who reads this today marvels at the panic it produced in his hearers. They imagine he must have ranted and raved as he spoke. "working the audience" as some preachers do today. But he delivered it quietly, from a prepared text. No shouting as you hear in "revival" preaching on TV or in tents in the summer across our land. His left elbow leaned on the pulpit and his left hand held his notes. No gestures; he stood motionless as he spoke. We're told Edwards did not usually try to evoke the kind of response that took place in the people who heard him that day. But this sermon was interrupted by outcries; men and women stood up and rolled on the floor, their cries drowning out Edwards as he spoke. Some people grabbed hold of the pillars of the church, so vivid was their sense of sliding down a slippery slope into hell.

Five years later Edwards published a book in which he said that "true Christianity is not revealed by the quantity or intensity of religious emotions but is rather present where a heart has been changed to love God and seek his pleasure" ("A Treatise Concerning Human Understanding," 1746).

Perhaps you are wondering what happened to grace in all this emphasis on God's judgment. I thought that God's grace was His favor to us that we don't deserve. How often we've reminded ourselves of Ephesians 2:8-9, "For by grace you are saved through faith: it is the gift of God, not of works lest anyone should boast." Then how can God judge us by our deeds, if we are saved by grace? Doesn't God's grace make His judgment impossible, since none of us deserves what He gives us freely? Nothing has disappeared of this grace.

I've come to see that the great truths are never to be seen only from one side. Somehow our salvation is entirely by the grace of God—

His favor that He neither expects us to earn, nor can we earn it. But God also holds us responsible for what we do after we accept His grace, through faith. Somehow it is both/and, rather than either/or.

Probably you would agree with me that it is dishonest in us to say we want God's love and forgiveness and acceptance, while we want to live as we jolly well please. We understand what James says in his epistle, "You show me your faith without works, and I'll show you my faith by my works." Paul, who wrote that we are saved by grace, not by works (Ephesians 2: 8-9) wrote in Romans 2: 6 that God "will render to every man according to his deeds."

Each of us has a nose to sniff out authenticity in others. We can't stand hypocrites—those scoundrels that deliberately say one thing and do another. "Walk the walk or don't talk the talk," we quip.

A recent Pulitzer Prize winning book by Frances Fitzgerald, "***The Evangelicals; the Struggle to Shape America***," spells out the story of what has become of the sector of Christianity that has its roots in the Great Awakening. I have lived through much of the story she tells, and I am troubled at how true her reporting is. The Gospel of God's grace has seemingly spawned a generation with less than holy aspirations.

Paul told us, "If we judged ourselves truly, then we would not be judged" (I Corinthians 11:31).

Dear brothers and sisters in Christ, do not respond to these thoughts with fear, but with determination to order, or perhaps, to reorder your life honestly before yourself, before others, and before God. Thankfully remember that Jesus came to save you, not to condemn you. Accept His forgiveness, and then be honest with yourself. Offer yourself to Him: follow Him, and you will never need to fear Him.

The Apostle Paul wrote to Timothy of "the crown of righteousness which the Lord, the righteous judge, will award to me on that day, and not only to me, but also, to all who love His appearing" (II Timothy 4:8). That means you and me.

It seems to me that it is to those who try to follow Him, but know they fail, that the message of grace makes most sense. To those who make no pretense of trying to follow Him, it is profitable to remember the judgment.

This is the word of the Lord.

Let us pray: "Holy Lord God, we thank You for Your grace. Grant that when we see our Lord, we may be happy at His appearing. Amen.

I Believe in the Holy Spirit
John 14:15-27

Shortly after I came here as pastor I called on one of our elderly ladies at Westminster Village. She was of a German heritage and asked me with a strong German accent, "Pastor Stuart, tell me what the Holy Spirit is?"

If I were to take a poll today to discover if you all believe in the Holy Spirit, I think everyone would say, "Of course I do." Some of you might feel it a slight, almost an accusation, to be asked the question. But if you were to answer Gerda's question, what would you say? I remember Mrs. Kohnke not only for this question but also because, though she was nearly blind, she loved to bake. She "demanded" that I taste her delicious cookies before I left. It was pleasant to oblige her; one of the perks of the pastorate!

Having said, "I believe in the Holy Spirit" what have we said?

I hope this morning that you will not simply leave here with a fund of information in your head. I hope you will realize that the Holy Spirit is not merely an abstract idea, but that He has come to minister to us in the deepest parts.

When our earliest Christian forbears said, "I believe in the Holy Spirit," they were affirming what every Jew believed, but had not thought of as an "aspect" of God. One of the first statements in the Book of Genesis is that "the Spirit of God hovered over the surface of the waters." The word translated "spirit" in Hebrew (*ruach*—ch as in Bach) is not capitalized, because in Hebrew there are no capital letters. It is equally well translated "wind." When we read this, we may picture something like a strong wind blowing over a lake. But when you read the opening words of Isaiah 61 you get quite a different sense from the same word. The prophet writes, "The Spirit of the Lord God is upon me, because the Lord has anointed me to bring good tidings to the afflicted." In that place "wind" would seem in appropriate.

In saying "I believe in the Holy Spirit" after expressing our belief in God, the Father, Creator of heaven and earth, and in Jesus Christ, the Son of God, we are tying together strands of information about God not tied together in the Old Testament. There is no doctrine of the Holy Trinity explicitly spelled out in either the Old or the New Testament.

Ancient Israel had read for generations about the Spirit of God hovering over the waters at creation. But they did not identify this "Holy Wind" or "Spirit" as a person of the God-head. The Israelites didn't have such a concept.

The sense that there was an extraordinary "something" that could be at work in a person was recognized long before Israel existed, in ancient Egypt. Genesis tells us that the Egyptian king asked after the Israelite slave, Joseph interpreted a troublesome dream, "Can we find such a one as this is, a man in whom the Spirit of God is" (Genesis 41: 38)? Dreams were of much importance in Egyptian religion. This Hebrew man that interpreted dreams must have in him the Spirit of God who sent the dreams. This is a different turn of phrase than "Holy Spirit," but it is as close as an Egyptian king could get to this idea.

The Jews knew well from reading Exodus every year in the synagogue about Bazalel, the architect of the Tabernacle in the wilderness. Moses wrote God's words: "I have filled him with the Spirit of God, in wisdom, and in understanding, and in knowledge, and in all manner of workmanship." When the Book of Job entered their canon, the Jews read Job's words, "The Spirit of God has made me." The great prophet, Isaiah, had written about One who was to come on whom the Spirit of God would rest as a "spirit of wisdom and understanding, counsel and might, of knowledge and of the fear of the Lord" (Isaiah 11: 2). Perhaps they knew of Ezekiel's words, "The Spirit of the Lord fell upon me, and he said to me, 'Say . . .'" 11: 5).

Persons speak; things do not speak. There was an extended interaction of the Spirit of God on Ezekiel, both speaking to him and lifting him (2: 2-15). So, the Holy Spirit was no new wrinkle of Christianity; God had shown this of Himself before.

But while recognizing clearly that this Spirit was from God, the idea of this Spirit as a participant in the God-head was unknown. The Jews believed in one God, a Deity that did not have the complexity of the Christian understanding of a triune God; three Persons, one God. The Spirit of God certainly came from God, but as an agent rather than as part of the Deity.

If Christianity contributed anything to God's people's understanding of Who the Holy Spirit is, it was because Jesus brought into focus the teaching that was already there. When we say, "I believe in the Holy Spirit," after affirming our faith in God the Father, and God the Son, we are simply connecting the Holy Spirit with the Father and the Son as Persons of the Holy Trinity—as Jesus taught us, though he never used the word, "Trinity."

This word was coined by the north African Church father, Tertullian in a work called "Against Praxeas." Praxeas was another theologian with whom Tertullian argued. In days when Christian ideas about God were not well developed, doctrines were worked out by close arguments.

Chiding Praxeas Tertullian wrote, not quite concisely, ". . . especially in the case of this heresy, which supposes itself to possess the pure truth, in thinking that that one cannot believe in One Only God in any other way than by saying that the Father, the Son, and the Holy Ghost are the very selfsame Person. As if in this way also one were not All, in that All are of One, by unity (that is) of substance; while the mystery of the dispensation is still guarded, which distributes the Unity into a Trinity, placing in their order the three Persons—the Father, the Son, and the Holy Ghost; three, however, not in condition, but in degree; not in substance, but in form; not in power, but in aspect; yet of one substance, and of one condition, and of one power, inasmuch as He is one God, from whom these degrees and forms and aspects are reckoned, under the name of the Father, the Son, and the Holy Ghost" (**Against Praxeas**, Ch. II, **Ante-Nicene Fathers** III, 598, Wm. B. Eerdmans, 1957).

Who was this Holy Spirit? Maybe you think I should have asked, "What was the Holy Spirit?" But "what" is improper because the Holy Spirit is a person and not an "it." You cannot grieve an "it, but you can "grieve" the Holy Spirit. Paul writes in Ephesians 4: 30, "Grieve not the Holy Spirit of God, in whom you were sealed for the day of redemption." He writes this after giving examples of what we should not do: speaking dishonestly, being unjustly angry, stealing, speaking in an evil way. These kinds of behavior "grieve the Holy Spirit" who is in us. When a married couple's unity is disturbed by harsh words, it grieves the wounded party. So, it is for the Holy Spirit when we live gracelessly.

We receive the Holy Spirit when we are baptized. This is a theological statement that may seem a "word" kind of thing rather than a reality. But there are mysteriously real things that accompany the Sacraments. I sense this something more each time I take the Lord's Supper. I don't see it, but I sense it. I feel closer to Christ. And though we see nothing happening at Baptism, the New Testament tells us something is going on.

In Acts 19 we read of Paul's meeting up with some disciples that included the highly regarded Christian orator from Alexandria, Egypt, Apollos. Paul asked them, "Did you receive the Holy Spirit when you believed?" They replied, "We have never even heard that there is a Holy Spirit." Paul replied, "Into what then were you baptized?" They replied, "Into John's Baptism."

Then we read, "On hearing this they were baptized into the name of the Lord Jesus. And when Paul laid his hands on them, the Holy Spirit came on them."

John's baptism that we read about in the Gospels was a sign of repenting from sin. This was different from what Jesus taught His disciples of a new kind of baptism. Jesus told His disciples, "Go therefore and make disciples of all nations, baptizing them into the name of the Father, of the Son, and of the Holy Spirit, teaching them to observe all things that I have commanded you" (Matthew 28: 19).

Baptism for Christians was an outward sign comparable to the sign of circumcision for the Jews. Paul did not explicitly say this, but in one place he puts circumcision side by side with baptism. For the Jews circumcision was a sign of being included in the covenant God made with Abraham (Genesis 17: 10-11). Paul wrote, "In him [i.e.

Christ] you were circumcised with a circumcision done without hands . . . you were buried with him in baptism, in which you were also raised with him through faith in the working of God, who raised him from the dead" (Colossians 2: 11-12)

Baptism was more than a sign of identification with Christ. It came with an accompanying gift of the Holy Spirit. In the Book of Acts, we read that after Paul put his hands on these twelve newly baptized folk, "they spoke with tongues and prophesied."

From this passage there has developed the teaching in some circles of Christianity about a necessary "second work of grace" after baptism, which is accompanied by the gift of tongues and prophecy. But here we read of something that happened on one occasion rather than of something that must happen all the time.

Paul wrote of gifts of the Spirit (Acts 10: 45) not to be confused, if I understand this correctly, with the fruit of the Spirit (Galatians 5: 22-23). The gifts of the spirit are given to fit people for tasks, as we read in I Corinthians 12. These tasks equip a person to be an apostle, a prophet, teacher, healer, helper, administrator, one who speaks in tongues, a miracle worker.

The fruit of the Spirit has, we might say, multiple flavors. It describes a sweeping inner reshaping so that one has "joy, peace, long-suffering, gentleness, goodness, faith, meekness and self-control."

When people are "ordained" for special tasks in the Church we lay hands on them in a public worship service and ask that by God's Holy Spirit they will be equipped for the needed gifts to do their tasks.

It may seem that nothing happens when we do this. However, I remember when I was ordained to the pastoral ministry, I felt that something had happened in me. Similarly, after a person intentionally "receives Christ" in an act of faith, the person may feel nothing, or perhaps she will. Some confess to a feeling of release, of shedding a burden, or maybe a touch of joy.

The Scriptures make plain that the Holy Spirit is a person. But, as we might expect of a someone who can equally rightly be called "wind," he is not limited spatially. He is as "ordinary" as breath, in a way. Paul wrote about "walking in the Spirit, not cultivating the works of the flesh." If we exhibit what Paul calls the "works of the flesh, among which are character traits we all reject, such as" strife, jealousy, selfishness, party spirit, and envy," it's as if we abandon the Spirit. If in a family member is dominated by these kinds of behavior, the result is a fractured home.

Conversely, when love, joy, peace, etc., preside in our homes, there is enduring happiness.

Paul is telling us that what breeds good things in our relationship with people is what succeeds in our life with God's Holy Spirit. That doesn't sound very theological, but it works. The Holy Spirit will both aid the disciplines by which we overcome unfortunate character traits and then live in us.

Perhaps you have encountered people that seem to have been taken over by evil. What they do shows an animating force that makes them cruel, selfish, hostile, etc. In a negative way this is parallel to being filled with God's Holy Spirit.

I remember once being asked by a pastor, "Are you filled with the Holy Spirit? I hadn't a clue how to answer. I think he was probing to see if I spoke in tongues. One can't quantify the Holy Spirit's presence.

What does the Holy Spirit do? Well, we have noted the Spirit of God hovering over the waters at creation. In I Peter we read that the Bible started to come together in ancient times as "holy men of God wrote as they were moved by the Holy Spirit."

The New Testament provides us many hints at how the Holy Spirit works, but I can only mention a couple key things He does.

He gives Faith. "Faith" is the principle product that the Holy Spirit "manufactures" in people. I heard recently that "having faith is like falling in love. Everyone is a candidate for it." But until a person sees the special one with whom he/she will fall in love, "falling in love has not happened."

We might say that the Holy Spirit does that special thing whereby that pestiferous little fellow whom you detested in third grade you now see in a new light when you are a senior in high school. Your eyes open; both your eyes open; you want to spend the rest of your lives together. In a similar way the Holy Spirit suddenly awakens in people who may have heard of Jesus for a long time a deep leaning toward Him. Until that something happens, Jesus remains just a name from the past—even for people who may have grown up in the Church.

He teaches us to pray. We probably don't realize it, but we pray because of the work of the Holy Spirit in us. Someone once told me that praying is "the breathing of the Holy Spirit in us." What is it that makes you shift from thinking, "I can do it," to "God, help me!?" What is it that makes you change mental gears from thinking, "Look at that magnificent sunset!" to "Thank God for creating the beautiful sunset."

He gives peace. Why is it that when you reached the limits of your endurance perhaps in a perilous situation in life, or as you were in the grips of a dangerous and painful illness and begin to pray (foxhole religion) that a deep settled-ness may have come over you. You didn't know why, but suddenly you felt the anxiety subside inside of you.

He awakens us to temptation to evil. Why is it that when you discover yourself tempted to do something wrong—perhaps being attracted to someone else's wife or husband, or perhaps to lie in preparing your income tax, or perhaps as a gush of gossip starts to gather in the back of your mouth—something inside of you balks and says softly, "Wait a minute!" Why do you feel bad after doing something wrong? We sometimes say it's the voice of conscience; but what funds our conscience? Where did it begin? Is it only a residue of culture?

He gives guidance. How does that peace come to us when we have to make big decisions, so that we know to decide this way rather than that? When our family moved to this city for me to become pastor, it was not long after we had seen the church I was then serving move into a new building. There were matters that distressed us, but I wondered if I did right to move. We felt a "preponderance of peace" in accepting the call to a new church that we took to be the reassurance of God's Spirit.

He is a presence in us. I could name so many other situations in life that you may not have thought of at all as the work of the Holy Spirit, but which show all the signs of the Paraclete's presence with and in you. The word "paraclete," translates a Greek word meaning "called alongside." The Holy Spirit is someone called alongside you.

The Holy Spirit is patient and gentle. He does not force Himself on us. When Paul tells us to "walk in the Spirit," he tells of a companionship that will alter our way of life. He will inhibit us from doing wrong and move us toward doing well. It is a privilege not just to believe there is the Holy Spirit, but to recognize how we are fortunate to have received this gift of God of Himself to us.

Let us pray: O Holy Lord God, our Heavenly Father, we thank you for the gift of Your Holy Spirit. Give to us His fruit and His gifts to do our Heavenly Father's bidding.

I Believe in the Holy Catholic Church
Deuteronomy 7:1-13; Matthew 16:13-19

Some years ago, after a service in which I'd led the congregation in confessing the Apostles' Creed, a woman in the congregation waited in line to tell me she was leaving the church because she finally recognized that I was taking it back into the Roman Catholic Church. She'd heard me talk about St. Augustine and St. Jerome and other "saints," a very Catholic word. Then it dawned on her what I was up to. Getting people to say the Creed, I made them take the final step and say it: "I believe in the holy catholic Church." Next week I'd be quoting the Pope as my authority. I couldn't convince her otherwise; she never showed up again.

Some of you have asked me why we say, "I believe in the holy catholic Church." Why not "holy Christian Church," as some Protestant bodies have rephrased it?

Before thinking about this very good question it is good to get some perspective on one part of the Creed that feels more like a wish than a fact, at least at times, and as we can see things. Our vision of ultimate things is more defective than it is of ordinary things.

There are those that distinguish between the "Church visible," the one you see, and the "invisible Church," the one you can't see. The invisible Church is the real one, composed of the "elect." The visible Church is a mixture of the "wheat and the chaff," a distinction that John the Baptist referred to after baptizing Jesus (Matthew 3: 12/Luke 3: 17). At the end of time the chaff will be separated from the wheat and burned.

Growing up in India I saw illustrations of this. Village women would take wheat that they raised or bought at the bazaar, put it into a flat basket with no rim on one side, raise the basket and let the wheat fall. The chaff, the husks on the wheat, would blow away. The grain they would grind to make *chapatees*, the delicious flat bread like what you have eaten in an Indian restaurant.

The earlier part of the Creed that referred to the judgment of the living and the dead refers to this. It is indeed a fearsome picture.

When we say, "I believe . . . in the holy catholic church" we don't go on to say, "that is, the wheat separated from the chaff." We just refer to the "holy catholic church." We do not here distinguish between a visible church and an invisible Church.

Jesus gave some severe teachings about the end times in Matthew 24, a time of intense tribulation, when antichrists would come to deceive many people. The parable of the sheep and goats that follows in the next chapter ends with those that do not respond to human need sent to eternal punishment (Matthew 25: 46). Mark's Gospel too writes of severe times to come, a great tribulation after which "the Son of man . . .will send out the angels and gather his elect from the four winds, from the ends of the earth to the ends of heaven (13: 26-27).

These are teachings in the Gospels we don't hear expounded much today. This is because, on the one hand, they are frightening images, not apt to be popular. On the other hand, no one really knows how to interpret these passages. They are there, and we should read and ponder them. They are part of Holy Scripture.

But when I put these fearful teaching beside the pictures of most of the teachings of Jesus and Paul, they seem to function as a ballast, a counterweight. In Matthew 10 we read some severe words Jesus spoke, "Do not think that I have come to bring peace on earth: I have not come to bring peace, but a sword" (vs. 34). This paragraph ends, "He who finds his life will lose it, and he who loses his life for my sake will find it" (vs. 39).

Jesus was often severe with the most religious of His fellow Jews, and least severe with the least respectable people. How gently Jesus speaks to the "weary and heavy laden." "Come to me and find rest. Take my yoke on you and learn of me; for I am gentle, and lowly of heart, and you will find rest for your souls. For my yoke is easy and my burden is light" (Matthew 11: 28-30).

There is danger for the preacher that attempts to expound on the frightening teachings of Jesus. Those that put strong emphasis on the idea of the "elect," that is, those that are in the "invisible Church," that will survive the final judgment, may be apt to think that they are in this favored body. And those who differ are the ones in the "visible church" that will be winnowed away at the last. Paul warned us all when he said, "Let him who thinks he stands take heed lest he fall" (I Corinthians 10: 12). He wrote this after retelling of his peoples' story in the wilderness when testing came in response to their grumbling.

The interpretation of the Bible in all its breadth is a fine science known only to the One who inspired those that wrote it. To those of us who presume to understand, well, we're out of our depth.

But I wonder if we are to take some guidance from the life of Moses, who led an often-recalcitrant people in the harsh circumstances after the exodus from Egypt. At one point in their impatience they induced Aaron to fashion a golden calf to worship. After this the Lord was so angry that he told Moses he was going to destroy Israel and begin again to make a new people with Moses, a new Abraham, so to speak.

Abraham bargained with God without success to spare Sodom (Genesis 18: 20-33). Moses persuaded God not to do destroy Israel and gave reasons that to us seem odd.

"O Lord, why does thy wrath burn hot against thy people whom thou hast brought forth out of the land of Egypt with great power and with a mighty hand? Why should the Egyptians say, 'With evil intent did he bring them forth, to slay them in the mountains, and to consume them from the face of the earth'." (Exodus 32: 11-12). He went on to say to God something that sounds bizarre to us, "Turn from thy fierce wrath, and repent of this evil against thy people."

Let us make clear what we see clearly, and not presume to explain what we don't understand. If we reasonably do not dare to speak to God as Moses did, we can at least intercede for the world as Abraham did for Sodom?

I am out of my depth here. But there does seem to be some parallel between the moment of God's severity in Exodus and what we read of God's response to human sin in the New Testament.

At the core of the Gospel is John 3: 16 that tells of God's great love for the world. So great was God's love that He sent His "only begotten Son" so that those that believe in Him will not perish but have eternal life. I have pondered what it means to "believe" in the first part of this study of the creed.

This has been a side avenue so pertinent to trying to understand what the Church is that I felt obliged to walk "where angels fear to tread."

The only Church we know is the one that we can see. The Church visible has suffered from some scandalous leadership over the years. Still today it is so. But the Church has offered much good to the world in a variety of ways over the centuries. There never has been a time when the holy catholic church looked ideal. Maybe as our Lord looks at us He sees a glorious bride, but as we see the Church it is full of spots and wrinkles (cf. Ephesians 5: 27). Paul wrote of a time when the Bride of Christ, for which He gave Himself, will be "without spot or wrinkle or any such thing," but the Church has never seemed so yet.

The quarrels some of us have with the part of the Church we know best are tiny reflections of the spots and wrinkles afflicting the Church at large over the past two-thousand years.

The problems began early. Perhaps we should see the problems ancient Israel had as the beginning of the woes of God's people. After Jesus came, things didn't improve much. I Corinthians tells us about a splintered church where the members piously quarreled over their favorite apostles, and maybe the most small- minded cluster claimed Jesus as its champion.

Paul had to address an ethical problem in this congregation of a nature worse than was tolerable in a port city known for immorality.

One of the big churchly snafus in the second century may have had a good outcome. A very devout and well to do fellow from northern Turkey came to Rome where he gave generously to the needs of the Church. He was an avid follower of the Apostle Paul who taught that the Church was no longer under the Old Testament Law.

This fellow, whose name was Marcion, took Paul's ideas and went for broke with them. The German theologian, Adolf von Harnack commented on Marcion that "He was the only one in the ancient Church who understood Paul . . . but even in his understanding he misunderstood him" (in F.F. Bruce, ***The Canon of Scripture***, p. 134). Marcion composed a collection of writings out of the Gospel of Luke and ten of Paul's letters that excluded all references to the Old Testament.

He so honored Jesus that he taught He was not a real man but was God disguised as a man. He took Paul's idea of the warfare between the flesh and the spirit to the extreme, teaching that the God who created the physical world was not the same as the heavenly Father of Jesus.

The Church in Rome kicked him out before he could distort the faith of the Lord Jesus beyond repair. But Maricon's gathering some of the early Christian writings into his collection may have helped to trigger the formation of the New Testament canon that has lasted.

When we read some of the writings of early Church leaders we are ashamed. A fourth century bishop of Antioch, known as John the "golden tongued," or Chrysostom, may head this list of troubling bishops. He went on to a higher office in Constantinople. Among the oratorically magnificent sermons he left to posterity are eight that are filled with vitriol against the Jews. Luther too uttered some horrendous things about the Jews.

Over the years some terrible things have been done by Christians in the name of Christ. The Crusades of the Middle Ages, which had as one of its cheer-leaders the saintly hymn-writer, Bernard of Clairvaux. When I sing his hymn, "Jesus the very Thought of Thee with Sweetness fills my breast," I can't imagine the writer of that hymn encouraging this blight in the history of the Church.

So, if the Church that we see is Christ's beautiful Bride, it's only as He can see it, and that by His grace. That Christ should think of us as holy, set apart for Himself, despite how we have been found through time and geography is a gift beyond generosity.

So, as we today try to understand the meaning of the two words describing the Church, "holy" and "catholic," perhaps we are asking how God can make a very flawed body of believers in Jesus into something beautiful as the Bride of Christ.

First, we should notice that the two words "holy" and "catholic" do not begin with capital letters—not that they would in the Latin original anyway. They are adjectives. They are not two parts of one name of an organization. So, when we say "holy catholic church we do not mean Roman Catholic Church. Though I am convinced that the Church with headquarters at Rome is as much a part of the Church as we are. We are two representations of Christ's Body that one day will be made whole. Perhaps we will recognize then how our disagreements were well intended illustrations of how meagerly we can understand matters beyond our experience.

Second, what does "holy" mean?

"Holy" simply means "set apart—in this case, for God. When God chose Israel, He said, "You are a people holy to the Lord your God; the Lord your God has chosen you to be a people for his own possession, out of all the peoples that are on the face of the earth" (Deuteronomy 7: 6). The next two chapters of Deuteronomy emphasize repeatedly that God did not choose Israel to be His people because they deserved it. They were not more numerous or more righteous. God chose them because He chose them, period.

We read an echo of these words in I Peter 2: 9-10, with reference to the Church. "You are a chosen race, a royal priesthood, a holy nation, God's own people, that you may declare the wonderful deeds of him who called you out of darkness into his marvelous light."

Then, echoing the prophet Hosea, Peter wrote of the Church, "Once you were no people, but now you are God's people; once you had not received mercy, but now you have received mercy."

This echoes what Jesus said to His disciples, "You have not chosen me, but I have chosen you" (John 15:16). Though Jesus didn't go on to say the critical things Moses said in the passage from

Deuteronomy 9, He might have. How flawed a body is the Bride of Christ.

Individual choice is so much involved in church life today that we have lost sight of the big picture that the Church is body of people that God has chosen.

A few years ago, a friend of mine, Nat Hatch, wrote a book that received some awards because he wrote it so well. But it was more than well written. It was prophetic. Its title was ***The Democratization of American Christianity*** (Yale UP, 1989*)*. It told the story of how from around 1780-1830 American Christianity moved west toward the Mississippi River and took on an identity quite different from the old denominations that formerly were the identity of American Christianity. It was a "groundswell that shook churches to the foundation" (p. 225).

The church split into many denominations with new names as charismatic preachers gathered flocks to themselves. Camp meetings turned into denominations. Christianity became another kind of democracy.

Much later the German Catholic theologian, Hans Kung referred, in one of his books, which one I can't recall now, to "the disintegration of Protestantism." It is an apt turn of phrase that has been oft paraphrased.

With our towns festooned with churches, we choose to attend this or that church in this or that denomination, or better yet perhaps, of no denomination. We choose to what extent we will participate in church life. We choose from an apparent variety of ways to live in response to the Gospel during the week— that run the gamut from "fanatic" to "token." So, it is difficult for us to think beyond our own experience to see that something bigger or more significant than the congregation we choose. To a lesser degree, since the Church is made up of people, personal choice has always been a factor in peoples' participation in the Church. But in our country this individualism went to new extremes.

Charles Colson has awakened many folk, including some from this congregation, to the fact that the Church is very much more than this in his book *The Body*.

We have accepted without blushing the fact that the "church" is another aspect of a consumer society. I know what Colson meant when he wrote: "Pastors feel the pressure to make the message as inviting as possible to draw people in. So, the process is gradual; a little rationalizing here. . . a little rounding off there." All of us live with the pressure to make the church "user friendly."

I have balked at being dominated by this way of thinking. We are a "holy" Church, a body chosen by God, a people separated for God. Not aloof, to be sure, in fact very much "in the world," but marching to the drum beat of the Cross.

While I agree that we are obliged not to be boring, and that we should "worship the Lord in the beauty of holiness," there is something serious about the Gospel. If we reduce the Gospel to attract people, we are not building the Church, but something else of slight eternal consequence.

Many years ago, Russell Conwell, who founded Temple University in Philadelphia and the seminary there that merged with Gordon Seminary in Massachusetts to become Gordon Conwell Theological Seminary, preached a sermon he called "Acres of Diamonds." He preached this captivating sermon thousands of times and wrote it up in a book. This was the first edition of the "prosperity Gospel," that later was to take over a popular segment of American Protestantism.

Conwell's message echoed Jesus' parable of the talents. "Use the talent lent to you; let it multiply and return it many folds to your Master." Russell urged people to "bloom where they were planted." The acres of diamonds were harvested as people applied themselves to work where they were. It was not a message encouraging greed.

The fruit of hard work need not be tarnished by greed. The Puritan ethic of hard work is a holy calling. Such work is worthy of a holy person. Should we become rich, let it not be because we used devious methods. And if we become wealthy we have the privilege of giving generously.

The modern prosperity Gospel follows a different line. It proclaims that a sign, maybe The Sign, of God's approval is God's shower of material blessings. Abraham was the premier saint of the Old Testament. He modeled faith, and God rewarded him bountifully. He became rich.

But the modern prosperity gospel I hear more resembles John Tetzel's marketing of Indulgences, than Jesus' parable of the talents. Tetzel sold certificates to get people out of Purgatory, with the proceeds going to build a new cathedral in Rome to honor St. Peter. Purgatory was the middle layer in a three-tiered universe, with heaven above and hell below. People that went to Purgatory after they died, could hope to get out of Purgatory into heaven. They were not so bad that they went straight to hell when they died. But Purgatory wasn't comfortable. It was a painful place.

The idea of buying Indulgences, certificates applicable toward getting relief from time in purgatory, was a development of the belief that there existed a "treasury of merit" made up of the excess virtue of the Virgin Mary, the saints and martyrs that one could draw on for one's own benefit. The check written to draw on this "bank account of excess virtue" was the Indulgence certificate. The Church was the bank, so to speak. A person desiring to reduce time in Purgatory could buy certificates good for varying periods of time, depending on how much money a person had and how much time he wanted out of Purgatory. In fact, one could buy these certificates for loves ones too.

The proceeds from the sale of Indulgences reaped a tidy sum for Pope Leo X to apply to the cost of the new St. Peter's Basilica in Rome.

But there're was still added benefit which made Indulgences of value. Not only would the sale of indulgences raise the money for the new cathedral, but it would also enable fearful people to reduce their time in Purgatory.

A very good salesman named John Tetzel marketed these certificates throughout the domain of the Church. But things got snarled when he sold them in Germany. Roland Bainton, in his biography of Luther, **Here I Stand**, tells us of Tetzel's sales gimmick. It was like some ads I hear on the TV. His hawkers sang out, "when a coin in the coffer rings a soul from Purgatory springs."

But in the German monk, Martin Luther, Tetzel encountered a buzz saw. Not only did Luther find the sale of Indulgences unfair, allowing rich people to afford more time out of Purgatory than poor people, but they also constituted a syphoning off money from humble German people to Italy. This practice amounted to a tax payable to the pope, perceived as an Italian prince.

The rest is history. Luther's protest of the sale of Indulgences led to the Protestant Reformation. And here we are half a millennium later with many churches whereas there was before only one church in the western world.

I am tempted to think that we are seeing facsimiles of John Tetzel's marketing technique in the hawking of a new Prosperity Gospel very different from the message of Russell Conwell. This aggressive plan for milking the needy is painful to see succeeding. The flaws in the church repeat themselves in each new generation.

The Creed says of us, we are "holy." This still only means the Church is set apart by God for His purpose. And that purpose will not be denied.

The second adjective we use to describe the Church is "catholic." "Catholic, with a small "c" means "universal," well, not exactly throughout the universe, but "world-wide." When we affirm belief in the holy catholic church we acknowledge that when Jesus said to Peter, "I will build my Church," He was expressing the purpose of His Incarnation. John's Gospel taught us, "To all who receive him, who believe in his name, he gave power to become children of God" (John 1: 12). We splice text with text to get a composite picture of Jesus' purpose. When He said, "I will build my Church and the gates of hades will not prevail against it" (Matthew 16: 18), we rightly couple that with John's statement, and that the "children of God"

John refers to are the members of the Church that Jesus builds. Its membership roll is known to Him alone.

At the beginning of each semester that I taught Church history at Purdue I asked the students to jot down on a 3 X 5 card why they were taking the course. The most common response was "to learn how there came to be so many different churches." It is hard to avoid the question, if you are a thoughtful person, "How did there come to be so many churches when Jesus prayed for His followers to be one as He was one with His heavenly Father (John 17)?

Why, over time, have so many of His followers found even the idea of unity in the Church so unappealing? The idea of an "ecumenical Church" is anathema to many, even though the word "ecumenical" means explicitly that for which Jesus prayed.

Today there are groups of people that believe in Jesus that think that they are most truly the Church. Their viewpoint has a history at least as far back as the sixteenth century.

N. P Feldmeth wrote in **The Encyclopedia of Christianity in America** (Intervarsity Press, 1990) that "[the] doctrinal hallmark of the Reformation implies that the individual Christian has direct access to God and the freedom to think, interpret, pray and minister independently . . . thus Protestants tend to be independent, and this. has proved to be both a strength and a weakness . . . On the negative side the Protestant penchant for autonomy has led to numerous denominational splits and a loss of unity" (p. 949).

Certainly, differences of point of view will develop when each of us loves God with all our mind, as well as with heart, soul, and strength. Indeed, I believe that we are unwittingly nourished well from the riches of our many different insights. Even "heresies" have had a place in furthering the Church's understandings just as dead ends in scientific research often lead to discoveries of value.

You argue, but Paul urged us to be "of one mind" did he not (Romans 12: 16), at least as we read Paul's words in the King James Version of the Bible. Indeed, it renders the Greek text exactly. But Paul meant, as the RSV and other recent translations have it, "live in harmony with one another." That's quite a bit different from agreeing about everything.

Jesus said, "I will build my Church." When you look around and see the plethora of disagreeing, different looking, different acting church bodies, think," that's the raw material of the Church." As you have seen building construction projects underway you never mistake a stack of bricks for the building itself. The pile of sand that will be mixed with concrete powder you know is just part of the raw material. Perhaps we should modestly see our own efforts at being the "real church" as just comprising part of the raw material.

There's only one such Body. Like it or not, we are just part of something much bigger than the worshipping community we like best.

I hear folk say, wryly, that when we get to heaven there are going to be a lot of surprised folk up there. What's he doing here? What's she doing here? A pastor friend of mine told me, with a twinkle in his eye, that down here we're Presbyterians, Methodists, Baptists, Catholics etc., but up there we'll all be United Brethren in Christ." Guess what his denominational attachment was!

I have a deep loathing for church competition, except perhaps in church league softball. This is the reason why I make very clear at every Communion Service that we celebrate "open communion." This means that people who have been baptized into Jesus' Body from the various kinds of Christian communities are welcome. This is because I believe when Jesus said, "I will build my Church," He meant what He said. We offer the Lord's Supper to all His Church.

I'm very glad that the Sunday in which I speak to you about the Church of Jesus, we are ordaining into His ministry four of our people whom the Holy Spirit led you to choose as elders and deacons. Your calling, deacons and elders, is to help us at Faith Church to build The Church.

While we're at it, maybe we should try to understand what "church" means.

Where did the word "Church" come from? The **Oxford Unabridged Dictionary** devotes about twelve columns to discussing the word. It may interest you to know that one derivation for the word that has been proposed is the Latin word *circus*, which means "circle." You say, that doesn't quite fit. Let's try another derivation.

More probably, the dictionary tells us, "Church" derives from the Greek word *kuriakon,* which means literally "of the Lord," and implied "House of the Lord." But that doesn't sound like "church."

The first Christian Emperor Constantine built several churches and called them "Houses of the Lord;" from that word in the plural form.

The word for "Church" we find in the New Testament is different. It is *ekklesia,* from which we get our word "ecclesiastical." This word, as commonly used back then, referred to the whole body of citizens in a Greek town, by contrast with the smaller circle of elected officials in the town council, the *boule*.

In the Greek translation of the Old Testament, in Deuteronomy 31:30, this word *ekklesia* is used to refer to the whole assembly of Israel, all the twelve tribes assembled together.

When you see the word Church by itself beginning with a capital "C," it refers to the body of all Christians; when you see it spelled with a small "c" it refers to a congregation. We are a church, but only part of the Church, a world-wide body extending throughout time past and future. It became world-wide originally when Jesus' followers accepted the "Great Commission." We need to be watchful that the Great Commission does not become the Great Omission.

What does Jesus look for in this Church He is building? What are the features that distinguish the Church from other aspects of society?

Calvin, the "grand-daddy" of us Presbyterians, taught that the Church may be recognized "wherever the Word of God is sincerely preached and heard; wherever we see the Sacraments administered according to the institution of Christ" (***Institutes*** IV, 1, §9). It is evident from the discussion that follows that he intended us to understand that a third "mark" of the Church is carrying out Church discipline.

I think that we may succeed in displaying the first two marks of the Church: I try to offer faithful preaching of Scripture, and faithfully to celebrate the Sacraments.

Our brethren across the Tiber River (Rome) think there are seven Sacraments, but I'm not sure Jesus worries about our quibbles on such things.

The third mark of the Church, discipline, is harder to maintain. As Calvin rightly says: "Because pastors are not always sedulously vigilant, are sometimes also more indulgent than they ought, or are prevented from acting so strictly as they would wish."

Charles Colson is persuasive in reminding us of the character of the fellowship we should look for in the Church. This inhibits the need for discipline, perhaps.

The fellowship of the Church guides us to bear one another's burdens and allows for real accountability. Accountability nips the need for discipline in the bud.

I have discovered that there is great capacity for wanting to bear one another's burdens. There's nothing that draws us together like recognizing the need of someone in the Church. You pull out the stops to visit the sick, to comfort the sorrowing, to give money when financial disaster has hit one of your own. I have watched this operate within our congregation.

But we are reluctant to accept our call for mutual accountability in following Jesus in difficult circumstances. We have bought into the tolerances at work in society at large.

I discover how independent-minded we really are when I or the Session steps over that boundary from giving "pastoral care" to "meddling" when someone crosses boundaries we all know are important. I confess that one of my great dilemmas as a pastor is coping with the awareness that "pastoral services" are thought of as pertaining to burdens to be shared, but not to reminding my flock of certain boundaries of Christian living. Colson has well said: "Sermons about holy living are empty exercises unless the church is willing to back them up with action" (p. 133).

Finally, may I remind you of something that has become increasingly precious to me about the Church. The Church is our true Home. When Jesus says, "Come to me, all who are weary, and I will give you rest," He is speaking the welcome of the Church. The Church is our true home.

When you come here. I hope you hear Jesus say, "Welcome home."

Let us pray: Lord God. we thank You that You have chosen us in Christ and included us in Your family. Amen.

I Believe in the Communion of Saints
Genesis 17:1-8; Acts 2: 41-47

I think some good people believe the "communion of saints," may refer to dead people that were very pious in life that meet in the afterlife to eat together the Lord's Supper. It's something they do together in heaven before we can join them. But it's not quite that.

On Friday evening as many of us mingled so pleasantly at our progressive dinner, it occurred to me how appropriate it is that I should be speaking two days later on the statement of the Apostles' Creed, "I believe in the communion of saints." Our fellowship two days ago is still fresh in your minds. You may even remember the menu and some of the topics of conversation. Without thinking about it we were mimicking one aspect of what we just read in Acts 2 of the community of the early Jerusalem followers of Jesus. Luke tells us their fellowship included "breaking bread from house to house." So did we, did we not? I suspect, however, that Luke is not telling us the early Church was one extended progressive dinner.

What do we mean when we say we believe in "the communion of saints?" Dietrich Bonhoeffer reminded us of how important is this community particularly during hard times in his little book, Life Together. Martyred just before Hitler's horrendous regime crumbled, Bonhoeffer wrote this small book as he nurtured an underground seminary of faithful pastors-to-be, who resisted the church in Germany that went along with the Hitler's Third Reich. Their togetherness was vital to their sustenance as they suffered for their faith.

When our forebears in Christ confessed the Apostles' Creed, they were not far removed in time from the ones mentioned in Acts 2: 42, whose communion (Koinonia) resembled the ideal economics of this early, non-Marxist communism. They had all things in common. The care of its orphans and widows was important enough to this community that they created a special office designated for this ministry, deacons. They met in houses to worship so they had no extensive capital investments to sustain.

When we say we believe in the Communion of Saints this confession is different from all the other statements of the Creed. On the one hand, it has to do with something Christ was forming, the Church, His Body on earth. It is also His Bride. On the other hand for His Body to be noticeable we must make this communion happen. It "really" exists, I suppose because Jesus said, "I will build my Church and the gates of hades will not prevail against it" (Matthew 16: 18). On the other hand, Jesus prayed as though this unity was something yet to be achieved, that "thou shoudst keep them from the evil one." Jesus prayed, "I do not pray for these only, but also for those who believe in me through their word, that they may all be one; even as thou, Father, art in me, and I in thee . . . that the world may believe that thou hast sent me" (John 17: 15, 20-21).

Another complexity of it is that, in one way, we are the entity called the Bride of Christ, "proposed to" by Christ, and thus married to Him. But in another way, as things have turned out, this Bride is a defective Spouse. We are visibly a dismembered Body though we are defined as complete, a single entity, the Church. Our splintered existence is what Paul referred to as our "spots and wrinkles" in Ephesians 5: 27, needing "cleansing by the washing of water with the word" in order to be presented to Him "without spot or wrinkle . . . holy and without blemish."

The early Church already showed the beginning of the problem. As I observed earlier in this study about the "holy catholic Church," there is resistance among Christians to the idea of unity. The term "ecumenical Church" is not winsome to many Christians, each group of which, clings to its unique identity. Each claims for itself a unique propriety, as though it has achieved Jesus' goal for His disciples. Some of the unique-nesses are a bit eccentric, but no less precious for that. Somehow, the aspiration to be one must arise in the Church so that "it," that is, "we" may want to achieve a positive answer to Jesus' prayer. As in God's ways with the Israelites, that He never forced them to obey His laws, so we are not compelled to obey the most basic aspiration of our Lord for the Church. We have to want it badly enough to discover what accommodations we ought to make with others who confess Jesus as Lord, but with whom we have differences we cherish more than we desire to be at one.

This desire seems to me implicit in confessing our faith in the words of the Apostles' Creed. In one sense we are disingenuous to say "I believe" with regard to either the "holy catholic Church" or "the communion of saints" if we know we don't even want to work to make these terms become descriptions. But in another sense I think we should keep on making these two affirmations as a pedagogical exercise even if we don't now want to become one with other Christians. Communion is something to be achieved, and we know it, so let's keep reminding ourselves of the goal by repeating often the Apostles' Creed.

This puts on us the responsibility of at least aspiring to something better than we have become. That we hope so is found in using the word Koinonia that keeps popping up as the unique fellowship of Christians. It is a Greek word, found in the New Testament, that we use as though it were an English word. I dubbed the church newsletter at the first church I served as a very idealistic young pastor, "Koinonia Nuggets." My people liked the word because it has a spiffy sound to it, and they knew its mysterious sound had significance.

Jesus could not have been more emphatic in desiring koinonia, that His followers remain one. Jesus taught His disciples, "I am the vine; you are the branches. Abide in me as I abide in you." The only suggesting of separating from the vine comes for branches that do not abide in the vine. Ironically, all those that separate from one another do so because they believe they are more surely attached to the vine than others. But Jesus taught that such a branch is to be "thrown away like a branch" and then "thrown into the fire, and burned" (John 15: 1-8).

As one of pastors of the church I now attend mentioned in a recent sermon, "A vine is a force to be reckoned with." It grows and grows so that it may take over a long fence line. Its branches increase, but all remain attached to the vine, and in doing so grow strong and send off new little buds that become branchlets, that become full-fledged branches. It goes on and on in a healthy vine. Thus Jesus expected would His vineyard community grow and bear much fruit. "My Father is glorified by this, that you bear much fruit and become my disciples." There is no hint of the fracturing of His followers that would ensue before long.

In His great "High Priestly Prayer" Jesus taught something that would be achieved as He demonstrated to them what leadership in the new Way was like. Since He would leave them, His followers had to continue the leadership and leadership style Jesus began. He demonstrated a kind of leadership unknown in the world. The leader was servant of all. He made this clear when He washed their feet, even Peter's, who protested; even Judas' who would betray Him (John 13). Where the leader is such an indiscriminant servant it is easier to be at one with others than if the leader wields executive authority.

John would write in his first epistle, "If we love one another, God lives in us, and His love is perfected in us . . . God is love, and those who abide in love abide in God and God abides in them" (I John 4: 7-21). This is not a sentimental teaching. John 3: 16 reminds us what this love cost God. "God so loved the world that He gave His only Son." And, as we know well, because we are reminded every Good Friday, when his Son came, His tenure ended with a very painful death, imposed on Him by a pitiless Roman governor.

While I feel awkward about Christian idealism that suggests we owe something to Jesus because He did so much for us, as though Christianity demands a quid pro quo, we ought to at least remember that our faith didn't come from rousing rhetoric by a eloquent politician. Such a one stimulates enthusiasm that may last for a while. The faith we claim accepts Jesus' quiet message, "If any one would come after me, let him deny himself and take up is cross and follow me. For whoever would save his life will lose it, and whoever loses his life for my sake will find it" (Matthew 16: 24-25). This is, I think, part of the price of Christian communion. A vast number of people from every corner of the earth that is persuaded to follow Jesus in this way has a bond that is very sticky.

Paul learned this lesson well from Jesus' disciples that taught him. Towards the end of his Letter to the Romans he wrote, "I appeal to you brethren, to take note of those who create dissensions and difficulties, in opposition to the doctrine which you have been taught; avoid them" (Romans 16: 17). My experience a pastor suggests to me that sometimes differences of doctrine come not always from clearer ideas, but often from personal animosities. In fact, when the doctrinal element is introduced, an insidious and disingenuous squabble may ensue. It may not be just about the doctrine. There is something mean about such a disagreement. If it were just difference of ideas, people that love each other will sort things out. Remember, what Jesus taught us was the chief point of recognition for His: John 13: 35, "By this all people will know that you are my disciples, if you have love for one another." And, 15: 17, "This I command you, to love one another." Followers of Jesus, because they lean toward each, as lovers do, may even grow stronger in their bond by sorting out their mutual lack of clarity on the deepest matters of faith.

But no one needs to remind us that this is not what has happened, since the beginning days of the Church.

To the Corinthian church Paul wrote, "I appeal to you, brethren, by the name of our Lord Jesus Christ, that all of you agree and that there be no dissensions among you, but that you be united in the same mind and the same judgment" (I Corinthians 1: 10). One modern translation puts some cosmetic on this appeal: "live in harmony with each other."

Our ire arises at the very idea of this intentional suppression of our personal opinions. So, Paul's teaching has been tapered to the lesser idea of having harmony, where we may even agree to disagree, in order to still remain friends.

The dissension in the church at Corinth was over who was the preferred apostle of Jesus, perhaps by whose name they should be known. Some said, we will be "St. Apollos' Corinthian Church," and others, "St. Peter's Corinthian Church," and the most contentious perhaps were those that said we are the "Jesus' Corinthian Church." Happily, when we claim the name of one of the early pillars of the Church, it is often not with schism in mind, but simply with making clear our connection to the earliest Church. I worship with a congregation that calls itself, "St. Johns." But this causes no dissentions with other churches in town. We are used to many denominations, and symbolically show our concord in principle by meeting together periodically. Discord presided among the members of the first century church at Corinth.

The earliest of the non-canonical writings of the early church was written toward the end of the first century AD. I Clement, was a letter from the bishop of the church in Rome to the church in Corinth that reminds the reader of I Corinthians, written by the Apostle Paul. This church had not sorted out its problems. We have no way of knowing if it ever did.

Very early on the seeds were sprouting that would develop into deep division in the Church. I want to probe a bit into the most difficult problem the early Church faced. This problem illustrates how difficult an achievement communion was at first. Then I want to briefly observe how minute are our reasons for sectarianism by comparison, that we are not able to overcome even though they are, by comparison, mostly nit picking. I fear our greatest problem is a lack of will power to take seriously Jesus' prayer for our unity.

The Council of Jerusalem described in Acts 15 was a necessity because of the honest difference of view of church leaders concerning a matter Jesus had not apparently addressed. They did not have access to Paul's Epistles to the Romans and the Galatians, because, of course, they didn't exist yet. Did Gentiles have to become Jews before they became Christians? Since all the earliest followers of The Way (as the faith that followed Jesus was called, cf. Acts 9: 2) had been Jews, it was only logical that non-Jews should follow the pattern: first become as Jesus was, a Jew, and then follow Him as did the Twelve, that were also Jews. This sounded quite reasonable, however awkward for male Gentiles that would then have to undergo the potentially lethal "surgery" of circumcision. From this pious but painful ritual infections often resulted. Modern antibiotics weren't available then, though I don't mean to disparage the excellence of much ancient medicine. Galen was no dummy about healing wounds.

One reason why there were many "God-fearers," throughout the precincts of the world where there were Jewish communities was that many Gentiles came to believe in the God of the Jews, without going through the steps of becoming converts. To become a convert, if you were a man, meant you had a series of steps to follow. First, you must want to become a Jew for no other reason than a deep desire to be joined to the community of those that worshiped the true God. Second circumcision, and third, a couple lesser difficult requirements: the ritual bath, complete immersion in the mikvah, and finally, make a contribution to the Temple. The mikvah was a ceremonial bath, a baptistery, we would call it, part of every synagogue, where Jews would be immersed for ceremonial cleansing after becoming ritually unclean. Women were ritually unclean after childbirth or menstruation. All people were unclean if they touched a dead person. There were other ways a person became ritually unclean. Women converts didn't have to undergo circumcision, of course, but only to be bathed ceremonially in the mikvah, and to make the contribution. God-fearers, for whom there was a particular name, theosebes, were respected in the Jewish communities to which they attached themselves, thought they did not go through the series of deeds needed to become converts. They could not call themselves "Jews."

So the early Church encountered the problem that the Jews had resolved quite easily, and apparently wanted to follow, but for one problem. The Church only had one category; either you were in or out. No halfway Christians as God-fearers were halfway Jews.

And there was a theological aspect to the main matter at issue: circumcision. Paul called attention to the detail that the covenant God made with Abraham, that extended his blessing to "all the families of the earth," was given to him before he was circumcised. Thus, he inferred, this extension of Abraham's covenant was offered to everyone that was not circumcised. In the place of circumcision, a new sign had been given to the Church, Baptism. It was painless. It could be offered to men and women. Its significance was profound, a sign of dying with Christ and being raised with Him.

Paul stuck his foot out in this line of thinking. There was as yet no Epistle to the Romans or Colossians that everyone could read. Thus there was not one biblical text about Baptism. Only what we call "the Old Testament," could be understood as authoritative. Nowhere in the Old Testament was "Christian Baptism" mentioned. It would have taken a small theological stretch to consider the story of the Syrian general, Naaman's bathing in the Jordan to get healed of leprosy (II Kings 5) as a symbol of Baptism. Had he thought of it, Paul could have pulled this off, as did at least three of the later Church fathers, Origen, Gregory of Nyssa, and Ambrose of Milan.

But at issue was not the rite of Baptism. There was no problem with that. Jesus had commanded Baptism as the sign of believing in Him. What was at issue was the right of the Gentiles' to belong in the Church, something that hadn't yet been figured out.

Paul, the last of the apostles was the theologian among them. This newcomer had not been a fisherman or a tax collector, but a professional persecutor, once a legal expert in reasons for getting after Jewish heretics, but now thoroughly transformed into an enthusiastic follower of Jesus. He had been a student of the greatest Jewish rabbi of that generation. As a Jewish theologian, he was a master of the biblical commentary called midrash. Midrash sought out the meaning of Scripture. It had rules of interpretation. The rule Paul followed was called qal wehomer, which meant "if it is true in the lesser, how much more so in the greater," or as modern expert in rhetorics would say, a fortiori. If Abraham didn't need circumcision before receiving the old covenant with God, how much more do Gentiles not need to be circumcised before being included in the New Covenant, not with Christ, but in Christ.

Paul saw in the covenant coming to Abraham before he was circumcised a detail with high significance. He didn't write this, but he might have said, "This was providential because God's plan all along did not stop with the genetic heritage of Abraham. Abraham begat a genetics of faith as well as begetting a family tree. God cared for all humanity, each one of whom was created in His image and likeness, a connection more profound than the generations of Abraham's family tree. Of course, Gamaliel wouldn't have agreed with the application of this passage in Genesis that Paul made, but he understood the principle. He had taught Paul the principle he used to arrive at this point.

Paul's teacher had showed his fascination with the new development in Judaism (Christianity) even before Paul was converted, well before he emerged as its leader. Luke tells us this about Gamaliel at a moment when the Jewish Sanhedrin in Jerusalem met to decide what to do with Peter and John who had healed a man in the Temple. Peter and John had not only healed a man, they also were preaching Christ to the people in the Temple that gathered around them after seeing this man healed. First Luke describes Gamaliel, and then reports what he said to the council.

"A Pharisee in the council named Gamaliel, a teacher of the law, held in honor by all the people, stood up . . . and said, 'Men of Israel, take care what you do with these men . . . keep away from these men and let them alone; for if this plan or this undertaking is of men, it will fall, but if it is of God, you will not be able to overthrow them. You might even be found opposing God'" (Acts 5: 34-39).

So, Paul, a student of the very thoughtful and kindly Gamaliel, had top credentials as an interpreter of Scripture. Did Gamaliel say these words in a private discussion "in chambers?" Did Peter and John hear him? We don't know.

But Peter and John, who did not have Paul's academic credentials, had clout in the early Christian community as members of Jesus' inner circle. Just as nowadays Christians with a fervent conservative bent are hesitant to change their minds easily, so it was then. If they have the stature of being among Jesus' early band of disciples, their opinions mattered, big time. So the Council at Jerusalem was a barn burner. It is interesting that at this council Peter first argued Paul's view, that Gentiles did not need to be circumcised to join the Church (Acts 15: 7-11). Peter led the way in this argument, and Paul followed (Acts 15: 13-21). This led, then, to the commissioning of Paul and Barnabas as the first missionaries, to go into Paul's homeland, Turkey. Paul showed his colors as he agreed on a major new issue with Peter, arguably the head of the disciples.

But an issue as great as this did not then die easily. Paul reports that later the controversy flared up again. There is anger, and maybe even a tone of jealousy in his "voice" that we hear in Galatians 2. After observing that a Greek convert to Christianity, Titus, had not been required to be circumcised, he wrote, "But because of false brethren secretly brought in, who slipped in to spy out our freedom which we have in Christ Jesus, that they might bring us into bondage" . . . [and then, pointing his finger at Peter he wrote], "from those who were reputed to be something . . . those, I say, who were of repute added nothing to me; but on the contrary, when they saw that I had been entrusted with the gospel to the uncircumcised, just as Peter had been entrusted with the gospel to the circumcised . . . when Cephas (Peter) came to Antioch I opposed him to his face, because he stood condemned. For before certain men came from James, he ate with the Gentiles; but when they came he drew back and separated himself, fearing the circumcision party. And with him the rest of the Jews acted insincerely, so that even Barnabas was carried away by their insincerity . . . I said to Cephas before them all, 'If you, though a Jew, live like a Gentile and not like a Jew, how can you compel the Gentiles to live like Jews?'" I wonder if it was as simple as this. Peter had learned backbone from his denial of Jesus three times on the night Jesus was tried. If he could later stand up to Jewish authorities after healing a man in the Temple, could he not stand up to his underlings, former Pharisees, that waffled on the idea of full equality with Gentiles? I sometimes wonder about the dynamics of some of these early controversies that are explained so simply.

Nowadays this early controversy is treated as though it was a no-brainer. But from what Paul reports in Galatians 2, we can see what a severe test this was to early Christian unity. His argument won the day. Now I know of no Christian bodies that insist on circumcision before they will baptize a convert to Christianity.

We think that any legitimate follower of Jesus should have known better than to think Gentiles had to become Jews first. After all, none of us modern non-Jews had to undergo this painful rite to become Christians. In fact, all we had to do was "come forward" at the end of the meetin', say the Jesus prayer, and we were in. Sign up and you're signed in. (Join the church, sign up to tithe your income and teach Sunday School . . . then, would you like to be an elder? We're having trouble filling all the seats on the Session.) But it was not so then. It was definitely not a no-brainer. With no precedent, how would one presume that a Gentile could leapfrog over Jesus' example to become a Jesus-follower? Jesus had been circumcised. Jesus celebrated the Jewish feasts. He attended the synagogue on the Sabbath. Go figure!

The early Church only gradually pulled away from Judaism. And it may have been that these early Jewish followers of Jesus, in rejecting circumcision for converts, thereby showed how they deliberately were separating themselves from Judaism. They were then effectively excommunicated from Judaism. The Gospel of John mentions the risk of being put out of the synagogue (John 9: 22), and Jesus told His followers of this act of excommunication (John 16: 2) as a risk they would have to face.

Did Jesus have in mind that His followers would remain faithful Jews as they followed Him? We'll never know. There were Jewish "evangelists" in those days that succeeded in making converts to Judaism (cf. Matthew 23: 15). Jesus' valedictory remark to His disciples echoed this centripetal force: "Go therefore and make disciples of all nations." Did he not say, "Truly I say to you, till heaven and earth pass away, not an iota, not a dot, will pass from the law till all is accomplished" (Matthew 5: 18)?

This did not mean that all the minute ceremonial laws and laws of purity would endure. What Jesus meant may have been what the great Rabbi Hillel meant when he was asked to explain the whole law while the one that asked the question stood on one foot. The Jewish organization, CHABAD tells the story this way:

"One famous account in the Talmud [i.e., the Babylonian Talmud tractate], Shabbat 31a) tells about a gentile who wanted to convert to Judaism. This happened not infrequently, and this individual stated that he would accept Judaism only if a rabbi would teach him the entire Torah while he, the prospective convert, stood on one foot. First he went to Shammai, who, insulted by this ridiculous request, threw him out of the house. The man did not give up and went to Hillel. This gentle sage accepted the challenge, and said: 'What is hateful to you, do not do to your neighbor. That is the whole Torah; the rest is the explanation of this—go and study it!'"

A later Christian might reasonably argue that Jesus was the fulfillment of all the law that mattered. After all, He dealt with the sin problem by His death and resurrection that the Israelite sacrificial system had to address in daily life long ago.

Peter and John continued to go to the Temple after Jesus resurrection. Other followers of Jesus no doubt did so too. It was the habit of faithful Jews. The gathering of Jesus' followers in Jerusalem at Pentecost (Acts 2) put them in the number of thousands of Jews that came there to celebrate this second of the three great Jewish feasts. It was a gradual drifting away that eventually separated Jesus' followers from the parent faith, Judaism.

Around AD 90 there was a Jewish council that pronounced a curse against heretics (Birkat HaMinim) that became the twelfth in a Prayer of Eighteen Benedictions. It would become, in time, twenty blessings. "And for slanderers [sectarians] let there be no hope, and may all the evil in an instant be destroyed and all Thy enemies be cut down swiftly; and the evil ones uproot and break and destroy and humble soon in our days. Blessed are You, Lord, who breaks down enemies and humbles sinners." This prayer is still recited three times a day by observant Jews.

The Jewish followers of Jesus were not the first to differ from other Jews. The Essenes were devout Jews that believed defective the piety of the Pharisees and Sadducees and every other stripe of Judaism too. Some of them lived in a separate community at Qumran on the northwest shores of the Dead Sea, while others, Josephus tells us, lived according to their careful rules in the towns that dotted Palestine. They expressed their convictions by lives lived according to their "Community Rule," while having the same Torah as the rest of Jews. There were other sects of Jews that remained under the umbrella of Judaism. The Way of Jesus, however, could not fit under this umbrella of Judaisms. It was not just that they believed Jesus was the Messiah. It was the other claims about Him, that he was the unique Son of God, that He was God incarnate, that were out of bounds.

There were other Jewish Messianic claimants over the centuries that drew followers, but were shown not to be the Messiah by their inability to regain the Jewish homeland and to bring peace on earth. In the second century there was a man that many around Jerusalem believed was the Messiah, Simon bar Kokhbah, but when he fought against Rome to deliver Israel, he failed. He and the great Rabbi Akiba, mentioned and quoted often in the Jewish Oral Law, were tortured to death by Hadrian after he utterly defeated the Jews. Then Jews were forbidden to live any longer in Jerusalem. In the seventeenth century there was a Turkish rabbi, Sabbatai Tsvi, who, caught up in Jewish mysticism, believed he was the Messiah. He drew a wide following. He was captured by Muslims and given the choice of converting or being killed. He converted to Islam. But his name lingered as well as his influence on Jewish mysticism, Kabbalah.

Judaism remained one religion despite its disparity of belief-systems. While some Jewish sects are noticeable because of their dress and their extreme exclusive behavior, to the outside world all Jews are just that, simply Jews. But when outsiders look at Christianity, they see the subtitles, Baptist, Lutheran, Presbyterian, Catholic, Orthodox, etc. I have students from conservative Protestant backgrounds who, in a classroom with a wide mix of religious bodies represented, refer to Catholics and Christians with no inkling of the oddness of the comment, or that they sound offensive to a number of their classmates.

I think "I believe in the community of saints" must be the most difficult article of the Creed to follow. It is easy to say, and perhaps to "believe." It has a welcome sound to it. But the Church has not been able to live up to it, which may mean that we do not believe it, really

In one way it is a definition of the Church. The Church is a "community of saints." By "saints" we mean people that are declared righteous because of Christ's self-sacrifice that paid the penalty for all our sins.

But I believe the intent of this article of the Creed was that it was not just a definition, but essentially a prescription for the Church. It is something to be attained. It should not be given up as a goal.

Its rationale is the wealth of teachings in the New Testament about Christian unity. There is one Body of Christ, we believe. Why is this so difficult to achieve? Maybe it is because the idea has to be a discipline as well as an ideal. When we are tempted to sever relationships with other Christians, how significant is the doctrinal issue? How great a tolerance do we have for small differences of view? Is there any sensitivity to a possible lack of humility when confronting "face to face" fellow Christians over mole hills magnified into mountains? Are we aware of matters that are essential by comparison with matters that are peripheral? What is essential? What is peripheral? What can we disagree on reasonably while recognizing that there is one essential, that we can confess together, "Jesus is Lord."

When Matthew's Gospel tells us that Jesus said, "Not everyone that says to me, 'Lord, Lord' will enter the Kingdom of heaven," can we let Him sort out who is doing the will of His Father in heaven, and who is not? And just in case the brother or sister that we suspect is not doing the will of our Father in heaven, is actually doing this will of our Father in heaven better than we are, let's give them the benefit of the doubt—and hope she will give the same courtesy to us. Humility is a Christian virtue.

As I began to ponder the article of the Creed about the Holy catholic Church, I remembered the person that left the congregation I then served because she believed I was leading our Protestant congregation into the Roman Catholic Church. Are we really still fighting the churchly war of early Protestantism? What if we had been able to speak with each other and listen to one another? Might I have alleviated fears that she would carry with her to another confrontation with another fellow Christian that could end peaceably? Might she have shown me that I was off center in my thinking?

Among the modern issues for divisions in Christianity one of the most frequently mentioned is the Bible, its authority and its inspiration. I am tempted to say that if the Bible is authoritative in the Church, practically speaking, it is not evident. The term, "the authority of Scripture" sounds pious indeed. But where are the goods? What is the evidence that it has authority? I hear impressive logical argument stemming from the idea of the Bible's Divine inspiration, but Christian behavior defies Christian dogma.

But all of our reflection on the Bible takes us beyond the boundary of the text itself. Indeed, every translation is an interpretation. One cannot translate anything without in some way being a "traitor" to what was translated. As the Italian proverb puts it, traduttore traditore, the translator is a traitor. The inferences we make from the Bible are from translations. Though we make much of discerning the context of Bible texts, our search for contexts most often extend only to the precincts of the particular book we read, or perhaps more broadly to the entire Bible. The latter investigation takes us into a vale of hermeneutics that often shows how meagerly we understand the texts, perhaps in the Old Testament, that we bring together with the particular text before us to form our interpretations.

In the years I have taught biblical Hebrew at Purdue University, I have been happy to see how many Christian students take all four semesters I offer, so that they can better understand the Bible. Some have repeated the second year since each year we translate something new. It is for many of them a devotional exercise, a discipline with high motivation. But many discover that once having dipped into the "original language," they are in an ocean, and the swimming is not as easy as in a backyard pool.

So some students go on to take courses having to do with the history of Egypt, Mesopotamia, and Israel, with Second Temple Judaism, with Rabbinic interpretation. They do this because the have become aware that there is the broader context about which they knew little to nothing before. They were goaded to enter this unfamiliar territory when they thought of studying the Bible "in context."

So, to speak of the authority of the Scriptures, if one presses a bit it is not hard to discover that from our devotional reading of the Bible, despite having prayed that the Holy Spirit would guide in understanding and applying what we read, we have to admit that we're not really sure what the "Bible says" about many matters.

Despite our lack of certainty on many things, once "democracy" infected the Church, these uncertainties morphed into points of view important enough to identify reasons for separating from one another. After the Protestant Reformation the Sacraments were a key point of argument. We split into factions based on our view of the Lord's Supper and Baptism. Strong leaders don't hold their certainties lightly.

The Marburg Colloquy (1529) I see often referred to as something of a watershed. Reformed and Lutheran leaders could not shake hands and leave as brothers because of disagreement about what happened at the Lord's Supper. Then "Anabaptists" were called that name because not having recognized the legitimacy of infant baptism, they required adult "believer's" baptism for its members, or Baptism again, that is, ana-baptism. Scots reformers detested the "black rubric" of having to kneel at the altar rail to take Communion because it suggested idolatry, that is, kneeling before the Communion bread and cup as though they were idols in the chancel. Good reason to split. Some Protestants believed one way about the end of times, when Christ would return and gather up His Church. Others believed differently. Neither knowing surely what Christ Himself did not know made no difference; their opinions were incompatible. On and on the disagreements unraveled the skene of good wooly Protestant Christianity, and the unraveling continued as a new way of being properly Christian.

Then there was/is this other matter: since we believe that salvation is by grace and not by works, we exercise selectivity in determining what "must" be obeyed and what is suggestive, but not required.

In some noble Christian circles there is great care not only not to do what the Bible forbids, but also only to try to do only what the Bible commands. These principles are most noticeably applied to ways of public worship. This kind of discernment was attempted among early reformers before the Reformation began. I admire the intense devotion of many of these good Christian folk, even though I don't live by their rule. Those I know seem to me to live faithful lives.

I intend no slight to Christians that have become divorced, a separation of a sacred bond that brings much pain. But the New Testament's teaching about divorce does not seem to be authoritative. If it were, it would seem that there would be far fewer divorces taking place between Christian husbands and wives than in the general public. I have read the statistics prove otherwise. There are, for sure, good reasons for some divorces, reasons that fit within the principles mentioned in the few comments that Jesus made about this human tragedy. If these were the only reasons for divorce, hopefully the precepts about mutual service and love would make most Christian homes sufficiently happy that couples would find home life a joy rather than a sorrow.

It would seem that Paul's exhortation to "overcome evil with good" would diminish the convincing appeal of the arguments of the gun lobby to defend yourself with firearms, even assault weapons.

I find it peculiar that if we follow the teachings of the New Testament we are deemed "liberals," while if we follow the current teaching in the most privileged democracy in the world, we are considered "conservatives." The mingling of "conservative" Christianity with "conservative" politics seems as natural as can be to those that think this way. How irate many of these well-intentioned folk become with those who are persuaded to follow the ways taught in the New Testament. Certain articles in the United States Constitution carry more weight than the authority of Jesus and His subaltern, the Apostle Paul. What an odd hybrid has evolved in American Christianity!

Does not the universal scope of the Gospel, and the explicit exhortation to show hospitality to strangers suggest to us that we Christians should fight against xenophobia, fear of strangers. If we bar them from our wonderful land of opportunity out of fear or because "immigrants" threaten our job security, by what biblical guidance do we further this behavior? My father was an immigrant; not from a third world country, but from Scotland in a day when good jobs were hard to find in his homeland. He was welcomed here, and found a home here. But he was white, and nominally Christian up until he became a "Christian for real." Recent studies have demonstrated that the Christians most eager to defend the authority of the Bible are in the vanguard of those that oppose immigrants finding a home here. It's difficult to see the biblical warrant for this unkindness.

When Paul exhorted us to be "of one mind," how aggressively do we strain to achieve this, rather than to submit to our differences and separate from one another?

As one after another pastor and priest, or other Christian leader falls to sexual temptation of the most miserable kind, child sexual abuse, or to virtual sexual abuse via the internet, what are we to think about the authority in Scripture having to do with sexual behavior? The intense harsh response to same sex issues has become for many church people a scapegoat. Having singled out one particular kind of sexuality to which the accusers are not prone, do they congratulate themselves? Meanwhile, there is strong evidence that the privacy of the home, and of the computer, has opened the door for many otherwise "conservative" Christians to become very liberal in their tolerance for sexual depravity. All this notwithstanding, we are earnest champions of the authority of the Scriptures.

This is a severe wound to the hope for the community of saints because in our human weakness we have not waled the hard road of entering the narrow gate, so to speak, of struggling forcefully against our human frailties. The authority of Scripture is for the purpose of helping us in the warfare of the flesh against the Spirit. But we must intend to win if the Bible is to have any authority for us.

So maybe it's good, then, to be reminded of the specific meaning of "saints." The term "communion of saints" comes from the Latin: sanctorum communionem. Three times in the last part of the Creed you see forms of the word: sanctum, or sanctam, or sanctorum. Each is a form of the word that means "holy." When we looked at the word earlier in this study we saw that it meant, "set apart." So as a communion of saints, we are a community set apart for Jesus." I propose to say "for Jesus" because we are an extension of that little group of twelve disciples and several women that were Jesus' intimate friends, walking together literally along the dusty roads between villages in the Jewish homeland.

The word "saints" has the connotation of "perfect people." But neither the word "holy" nor the word "saint" means "perfect." If it did, why did Jesus teach His disciples to pray, "Forgive us our debts (or trespasses or sins) as we forgive our debtors." As a communion of saints, we are about as far from perfect as east is from west. One of few bumper stickers that I chuckle at rather than scowl at reads: "Please be patient; God is not through with me yet." Me too.

To say I believe in "the communion of saints means, "I believe I have a place in a community set apart for/by God." I wonder how that sounds to you as a description for the life of a church: The mutual participation of people set apart for/by God.

The Book of Exodus includes God's word to Israel that they were a "communion of saints," that is, of people uniquely chosen by God. In Exodus 19: 5-6 we read of Israel's uniqueness: ". . . if you will obey my voice and keep my covenant, you shall be my own possession among all peoples . . . and you shall be to me a kingdom of priests and a holy nation." The Hebrew word for "possession" (segula) here is rendered in the old KJV, "peculiar treasure," that is a bit more picturesque than "possession." But it began with an ethnic identity that Israel had in its relationship to Abraham. Christianity has no ethnic glue.

But Abraham's role in the great scheme was not limited to his genetic descendants, Israel. Paul, in Romans 4: 11 made the point that God's promise to Abraham came before he was marked with the sign of the covenant, circumcision, that would identify his descendants. So the promise pertained to everyone who, like Abraham, would trust in God. So the "communio sanctorum," the communion of saints composed of "set apart ones" did not have this ethnic boundary. Those of us who were not born into that privileged lineage of Abraham's physical descendants are as included in the covenant with Abraham as are his physical heirs.

In the New Testament we find the term in Exodus 19: 6, "Kingdom of priests and a holy nation" used with reference to Christians too. I Peter 2: 9 aligns us who are Gentiles with Abraham's heirs: "You are a chosen race, a royal priesthood, a holy nation, God's own people, that you may declare the wonderful deeds of him who called you out of darkness into his marvelous light." So now the idea of this sacred society, sacred because chosen by God, has bloomed. Indeed, Abraham's purpose was that "in him all the families of the earth would be blessed" (Genesis 12: 3).

I think that many of us have a foggy sense of what we owe to Abraham. This is our heritage, our tradition. Jaroslav Pelikan has made a life's work of studying how important this tradition has been for us. This heritage has worked into us even though we don't recognize it. Pelikan drew on the Polish Nobel Prize Winning poet,

Czeslaw Milosz, in addressing this point. Milosz wrote,"'Certainly, the illiterates of past centuries, then an enormous majority of mankind, knew little of the history of their respective countries and of their civilization,' and yet their lives were decisively shaped by that history" (The Vindication of Tradition, Yale UP, 1984, p. 19). This is true of us Christians too, as heirs of our forebears. Even though you may have zero sense of your connection to Christians who lived before you, they were the ones who passed along to you the Gospel which is precious to you.

Our "communion" involves us in a fellowship with all Christians from the past, the present, and with those yet to be born. If we know all the irritants that Christians of the past might offer us, about which we know nothing, perhaps we'd not be quick to claim this kinship with them. But we don't know of this, and so we gladly claim the idea of their kinship.

The problem with the past, however, is more than hypothetical for many modern Christians. Many refer to our sacred heritage with something of a scowl, even referring to it as "dead tradition." But Pelikan made the quotable comment that "Tradition is the living faith of the dead, traditionalism is the dead faith of the living" (p. 65). What they passed on to us was everything we know and trust as the substance of our faith. There are those with a "dead faith" that are locked into "modern" traditions, perhaps locally devised, and of recent vintage. Their habits are not ancient, but are binding. It's what they are used to. What they are used to has not fed into a vital life of faith.

The communion of the saints is a relationship with the past as well as with the present, whether or not we recognize the roots of our faith. The passage from Genesis we read today about Abraham, and the other in Hebrews 12 that tells us of the "great cloud of witnesses," that surrounds us, tell us what we owe to this continuity reaching back to Abraham. We sing "For All the Saints" with immense gusto, glad for the truth it brings to our mind. In the days when churches had graveyards beside them for their departed saints, Christians could look out the window on the Lord's Day and be reminded of their "cloud of witnesses," that grew as their beloved elderly folk passed away.

This communion is not only what we enjoy now, but also a mysterious, invisible fellowship from which we can take comfort when we are distressed by the realities we see in the present condition of the Church. That is, our most pressing problem in maintaining a sense of communion of saints is all the participants in "churchianity" that we think don't belong. I have sometimes felt bad in knowing I was not welcome at the Lord's Table with fellow Christians who were intent on guarding the integrity of their discipline by serving "Communion" at a "closed table." Being denied access to the Lord's Table may be because of doctrinal niceties that the denying church deems essential to true faith.

St. Augustine saw Noah's ark as a figure of the Church. He wrote: "God commanded him . . .to make an ark, in which he might be rescued from the destruction of the flood . . . as a figure of the city of God sojourning in this world; that is to say, of the church, which is rescued by the wood on which hung the Mediator of God and men, the man Christ Jesus." (City of God XV, 26, p. 206, Nicene and Post-Nicene Fathers, Vol. II, Grand Rapids, MI, Wm. B. Eerdmans (1957).

Augustine did not draw this idea from the illustration of Noah's ark, but he might have noted that this ark, this picture of the Church, was filled with animals of many varieties.

Augustine resisted forcefully one of the schismatic groups of Christians in North Africa because they rejected the consecration of a bishop over the diocese of Carthage because one of the bishops taking part in his consecration had been a traditor. That is, during a period of persecution, fearing for his life, this bishop had given over sacred books to the persecutors. Those that rejected the suitability of this bishop felt that his participation was warrant for breaking away and forming a new church. They followed their bishop, Donatus, out of the Church for reasons of purity.

This crisis in the north African Church illustrates a problem that has continued to cause divisions in the Church. Christians may disagree on many matters. Many of these matters are important to both sides of the argument. They have to do with definitions of the inspiration of the Bible, with the boundaries of sexual behavior, with matters of church government, with matters pertaining to when Christ will return, with matters of style of worship. But which of any of these reasons trumps Jesus' plea for our community, or with Paul's chiding of the Corinthian church for its sectarians various claims for superiority over other groups in their church?

While it is understandable that churches living far separated geographically from other churches should develop ideas differently, so that they don't violate the teaching of our Lord about Christian community. We cannot plead this reason for our schisms, often promoted with an apparent sense of being obedient to Scripture. Schism has become a new virtue in Protestantism.

Even within the bodies that have pulled away from their former community for reasons of doctrinal or sexual purity, scandals have hurt the perception of the Church in society. The list of conservative Protestant leaders that have fallen conspicuously has given reason for outsiders to scorn all the protestations of superior morality in the Church. The Catholic Church as well as the Protestant churches has hurt the image of the Church with its litany of fallen priests and bishops allowed to keep on until reaching a nadir of shame.

It is no claim to freedom to sin, but seems so, that we should claim the Communion of Saints is made up of those for whom the grace of God is needed extravagantly.

This is a hard matter because it is true, a church may become like the church in Laodicea, mentioned in Revelation 3: 14-22, while still being called a church. To it Christ wrote, "because you are lukewarm . . . I will spew you out of my mouth." But it was to this church that Christ said something we love to repeat, "Behold I stand at the door and knock; if anyone hears my voice and will open the door, I will come in to him and eat with him, and he with me." Which tells us, I think, as we survey the surrounding claimants to being Christians, and estimate those persons or bodies with whom to "communicate," we should let One judge this matter whose vision is clearer than ours and whose invitation is clearly more cordial than ours. A day will come, I've often heard it said whimsically, when we'll look around us in heaven and wonder how (in the heck?) this one and that one got in. And, of course, these will be no doubt exclaiming the same thing about us.

We need to remember Paul's appeal: "Walk worthy of the calling with which you have been called" (Eph. 4:1). Hear that lingering appeal: "Walk worthy of the high calling with which you have been called." It is never to be a presumption of superiority, but always a call to a way of life. For sure, Christians have no reason to feel superior in any way. We all can say, as Paul said of himself, "The good that I want to do, I don't do; the bad I don't want to do, I do" (Romans 7). Everyone can echo Paul's confession. But this, then, is no reason to stop trying.

The battle is so gradual, as though what is at issue is only a choice between alternative and equally adequate "styles" of Christianity. We assign labels to our sides of issues, "conservative," or "progressive," or perhaps something more precise. These labels get us into some muddled thinking. Each had its own expectations; compromise was defeat.

But sometimes the conflict is needful. Many years ago, in Germany, Dietrich Bonhoeffer discovered that Christians in his country faced what he called "battle conditions within a hostile state." Already as a young man he was forced to re-think being a Christian in a country where the State allowed only a kind of Christianity to be practiced that fit in with the ideals of a State ruled by the ideology of one man, Hitler. It was a life and death struggle. With his talent, family background, and good looks, Bonhoeffer could have climbed to great heights in the "churchianity" of Hitler's Germany. But he would not because he was a "saint," a Christian, a person set apart for/by God. He recognized, as he put it, that Christianity "is not about abstractions but about actual life."

This new gathering with which Bonhoeffer identified came to be known as the "Confessing Church." Several of the leaders of this Confessing Church were executed by Hitler, and there were some people in the state church who thought they deserved to be.

Looking back on that generation, you and I can see clearly what Bonhoeffer and many other Christians of his generation in Germany saw. We admire their courage and their devotion to Jesus. They were right.

In the last book of the Bible, Jesus addresses a church in the prosperous city of Laodicea in Asia Minor. "I know your works; you are neither cold nor hot. Would that you were cold or hot! So, because you are lukewarm, I will spew you out of my mouth. For you say, I am rich; I have prospered; I have need of nothing. . . Therefore, I counsel you to buy from me gold refined by fire, that you may be rich, and white garments to clothe yourself, to keep the shame of your nakedness from being seen, and salve to anoint your eyes, that you may see. Those whom I love, I reprove and chasten; so be zealous and repent. Behold, I stand at the door and knock; if anyone will hear my voice, and will open the door, I will come in to him and eat with him and he with me."

I believe in the communion of saints. It is a goal to be sought after. It is an identification defined by Jesus in His kindly invitation, "Come, follow me."

Let us pray: O Lord, explain to us so that we can understand that we have been set apart for You. Draw us then together to be and do what you have taught us. Amen.

I Believe in the Forgiveness of Sins
I Kings 8:33-40; Matthew 18:21-34

One of the best-known stories in the Gospel of John is probably remembered widely because of one sentence Jesus said. It is the story of the adulterous woman caught red-handed. A group of religious leaders brought her to Jesus and placed her before Him. The Law of Moses, they told Jesus, required that a woman caught in adultery was to be stoned to death. The Law found in Leviticus 20: 10 and Deuteronomy 22: 23 states that if a man and a woman are caught in the act of adultery both are to be put to death. Stoning is not specified. Death by stoning is the sentence for a young woman, engaged to be married, who is found not to be a virgin (Deuteronomy 22: 21). The accusers of this woman were legally off base. Had they been concerned for the Law of Moses the man with whom she cohabited should have been present for condemnation too. They had in mind to find reason to accuse Jesus of being soft on the Law of Moses. Ironically, they were the ones that were soft; they didn't know the Law.

When I read of an incident like this that involves Jesus' purported violation of biblical law, I wonder what the Jewish practice was on the issue in question in his day. The religious leaders described here far exceed the practice of Judaism in Jesus' time.

The **Mishnah**, the written form of the Jewish oral law, that had begun to develop during the time of Ezra but was written down in AD 200 lets us know the point of view of the rabbis on this issue. This quotation is from tractate Makhot 1: 30. "A Sanhedrin that executes once in seven years is called bloodthirsty. R. Eleazar b. Azariah said: even once in 70 years. R. Akiba and R. Tarfon said: had we been in the Sanhedrin, none would ever have been put to death. Rabban Shimon ben Gamaliel said: then these sages would have created more murderers in Israel."

That Jesus should have been reluctant to pass sentence of death on this woman puts him square within the views of rabbis most respected before and in his time.

But this story is not about the Law of Moses but about something else. This something else was, to put it generously, the hypocrisy of the women's accusers. Jesus' oft remembered reply to them, as he wrote with his finger in the dust: "Let him who is without sin among you be the first to throw a stone at her" made her accusers melt away (John 8: 7).

This one sentence Jesus spoke has echoed in many a religious circle perhaps for the wrong reason. Jesus didn't excuse the woman. He did not say "to sin is only human." Jesus' words did not teach us that sin is no big deal, so that we can be excused for the sins we are prone to commit. He called what she had done "sin."

This story is not really about forgiveness. Jesus didn't say to her, "I forgive you." He said, on noticing that the woman's accusers had disappeared, "Neither do I condemn you. Go and do not sin again."

What this story does illustrate is a characteristic in human nature that these religious leaders exhibited in the extreme: the capacity of ordinary sinners (like me) to judge someone else harshly even though he knows he is a sinner too. That these were religious leaders should not surprise us. Indeed, the infamy of certain religious leaders in our day that are known for their keen critique of the sins of others reminds us that this is a common lesion in the consciences of even the moral rudders in a society. The pointy-fingered religious authority figure, ferreting out the peccadillos of others, meanwhile posing as righteous, merits the scorn people instinctively feel toward him. But this should not make us get soft on moral goodness itself.

This story does not appear in the Gospel for the benefit of judges, but for the benefit of us all. We are not to stand in judgment of one another.

But, this idea too may be misused. While it is true that we are not appointed as judges of one another, each of us is accountable to God. In telling the woman that he didn't condemn her, and urging her to go and sin no more, perhaps Jesus knew that the accusation against her was legally defective. The man complicit with her was not there, so the case would be thrown out before the Jewish court. Jesus acknowledged that she had "messed up." He told her to go and sin no more, which meant to her, "don't commit adultery anymore," not "never commit any sin again." This was beyond her ability as it is for us too.

For most of us, the condemnation we have in mind for others is inappropriate. The offense seldom involves breaking a law of God, but simply something that irritated the other. A principle I think of often: "Be reluctant to be offended; be sensitive to offending others."

Today before us is the statement in the Creed, "I believe in the forgiveness of sins." What are we saying? I think that the meaning of this statement of faith is broad.

Think back to the first story about human beings in the Bible. After we read of the disobedience of our first parents in the Garden of Eden, their relationship with God was affected, their relationship with each other was affected, their inward peace was affected, and nature was affected.

They went from pleasant walks with God in the Garden of Eden to being expelled from that paradise. In the end they would die just before the end of the day, that is, thinking of a day as one thousand years (Psalm 90: 4). When God spoke to Adam, as Adam hid in some lush grove in paradise, asking him how he knew he was naked—a word that should not have been in his vocabulary, Adam blamed his bride. Now Adam and Eve discovered this troubling capacity called conscience, that often eroded inner peace. They now knew the difference between right and wrong, and of their tendency to do both. Not only this, but now the ground would be hard to cultivate, and childbirth would be painful. The effects of the first disobedience were catastrophic.

Does forgiveness of sin apply to the undoing of all this catastrophe? The forgiveness of sin restores all this brokenness that is a result of the first disobedience. The last book of the Bible tells of a new heaven and a new earth. This is the final act of God's forgiveness, restoring the cosmos.

One way that we reflect the image of God is in the ability to feel wronged or sinned against. But we are like the ones that brought a "sinner woman" to Jesus, expecting Him to condemn her. While offending others, we are too often insensitive to the offenses we impose on them.

A way in which we reflect the brokenness of the image of God in us is the distress we feel at our mistreatment of ourselves, when once we realize it. The guilt we feel from letting ourselves down, not living up to what we think we ought to be, reflects this feeling of offending ourselves. This too needs forgiveness.

The forgiveness of sin is the whole purpose of the Gospel. God's project of forgiveness aims at restoring all this brokenness, from the broken relationship with him to the healing of the cosmos.

When we are forgiven and offer forgiveness it makes gracious society possible. From a person's standpoint, it offers peace within, fulfilling Jesus' promise: I came that [you] may have life abundant" (John 10: 10).

In giving His Son to die to pay the penalty for our sin, God completed a development of response to human sinfulness that began severely in the third of the Ten Commandments. There God extended the penalty for worshiping idols to "the third and fourth generation" (Exodus 20: 5).

This extension of penalty for sin was reduced as Jeremiah and Ezekiel spoke for God. "Everyone shall die for his own sin" (Jeremiah 31; 30). Ezekiel amplified this promise, "The soul that sins shall die. The son shall not suffer for the iniquity of the father nor the father suffer for the iniquity of the son; the righteousness of the righteous shall be upon himself, and the wickedness of the wicked shall be upon himself" (Ezekiel 18: 20).

The penalty for offenses against God were reduced further among the devout Essenes in their community at Qumran. **The Damascus Document** found among the **Dead Sea Scrolls** simply expels people for the kind of offenses that the Hebrew Bible stated were worthy of death. "If it is a matter deserving death, then they shall watch him, and he shall never come back" (Michael Wise, et., al, ***Dead Sea Scrolls, a New Translation***, "The Damascus Document," 4Q266, Fragment 18, Column 4, [HarperCollins, 1996], p. 72).

But when Jesus came for us, He did something that had not been possible before. He took on Himself the penalty for all our sin. So that in the Creed, we can say "I believe in the forgiveness of sin."

But the Creed does not spell out the benefits, the sweep and the reason for this forgiveness. That is for us to ponder. The purpose of forgiveness is to reconcile us with God, with one another, with ourselves, and with this earth that God created and called "very good."

That term, "fellowship with God" may seem like only a pious turn of phrase. But there is something to it. I don't think that it implies a requirement to become a mystic. Fellowship with God seldom comes, I think, from trying hard to achieve it by excesses of Bible reading, prayer, or ascetic acts. Instead, it comes unexpected when the right pieces are together in us in the puzzle of life.

When Jesus taught us in those words that come after the Lord's Prayer, that if we do not forgive others their trespasses against us, neither will our heavenly Father forgive us our trespasses against Him, because fellowship with each other is part of fellowship with God. We can't have fellowship with God if we are out of sorts with each other, and it's our fault.

The need for forgiveness is like the need for oil to keep a delicate machine running. The machinery of a family, or of a congregation, or neighborhood needs the oil of forgiveness to survive happily.

An impression that has come to me frequently as a pastor is that it is very difficult for people to confess to each other wrongs they have done, while feeling offended if others do not confess their offenses against them. The prayer of confession of sin that we often say in worship on the Lord's Day is called on to perform a greater task than it was cut out for. It does not cover all the bases needing to be covered. We are reminded to confess our sins when we repeat this line in the Lord's Prayer, but we need to follow up by acknowledgement of our offenses against others.

I wonder how many people sitting in the pews on any given Sunday morning are languishing because they are unable to confess wrong they have done. They are too proud, or they think that to admit an offense will tarnish their image. Meanwhile, the lines of friendship and community are broken by this cross fire of inability to confess. I think we all might be apt to forgive quickly many offenses if we heard a humble word of confession from the one (s) that offended us.

Some, I think, don't apologize because they don't believe they have offended. Or, if they know they have offended they believe that the other needed to be put in his place. They deserved to be offended as a rebuke.

Perhaps their consciences are unable to detect their offenses because they see apologizing as a sign of weakness. Others have overly weak consciences but because they see few examples of mutual confession in their church they fear their apology won't be accepted. So, they sink into a marsh murky with guilt, perhaps hoping the public and formal confession of sin in saying the "Lord's Prayer," will provide relief—but seldom does.

This, then feeds into the fourth layer of need for forgiveness, the ability to forgive myself. This may be the most painful level of the lack of forgiveness. I owe the forgiveness to myself, but I am not able to give it or receive it. Those that have often been rebuked by their parents during childhood are susceptible to the inability to feel forgiven.

Jesus died on the cross to make forgiveness possible. Jesus' forgiveness can act like an eraser, wiping away with one sweep the sin that burdens us. The inability to accept and to feel forgiven from God, from one another and from ourselves hinders us from enjoying the peace that comes with knowing that in Christ we are forgiven.

The Church (and the church) suffers a needless neurosis as a consequence. God is larger of heart than not to forgive us even our sense of need for forgiveness that has become atrophied.

I also think that Jesus' words about the requirement to forgive one another to receive God's forgiveness may be a warning rather than a threat of eternal damnation. The psalmist tells us, "He knows our frame; He remembers that we are dust (Psalm 103: 14).

Sin?

But there is another piece to this equation of sin and forgiveness. What do we have in mind in saying "sin?" We sin when we violate the Divine law, the laws spelled out in the Ten Commandments. Happily, we are not held accountable for violating the ceremonial laws of the Old Testament. But the New Testament comments on sin too.

The "Sermon on the Mount," for example, contains "Beatitudes" that are not mere suggestions. These set forth Jesus' idea of goodness. Half of Paul's epistles are composed of precepts for Christian life.

Romans 12 tells us we are to bless those that persecute us, rejoice with those that rejoice, and weep with those that weep. There are numerous such precepts of the Christian life that we commonly treat as suggestions of how to be a gung-ho Christian, but surely not for the rank and file Christian. After all, we're only human.

Romans 1 is often mentioned for its rebuke of a kind of sexual practice that many devout folks consider the nadir of human sins. Yet in that same passage Paul itemizes other offenses, including envy strife, deceit, malignity, gossip, slandering, insolence, heartlessness, ruthlessness that come because of "not acknowledging God" (12: 28). We are selective in our recognition of what is sin. In doing so we do not include these offenses of which we may be prone in our request to God, "forgive us our sin." Many of these offenses are "just part of human nature." Some of us are disposed to a hair-trigger temper, or to hastiness in telling others tasty tidbits of the scandals they've heard. We don't call it gossip, when we do it, but it's just that.

We attribute our reflex of temper to our Irish background, or some other genetic predisposition. But the sum of these offenses, unconfessed and unforgiven, is damaging to the Church, to our friendships, and to our own inner well-being . . . and to how we treat the earth on which we live.

There are offenses we receive from others and extend to others. These are sometimes "misunderstandings," but they seem to those that we offend on a par with sin. There are unintended as well as intentional offenses, whether against God's laws or against one another.

We offend ourselves. A life without order or dignity is an offense to the one who lacks these qualities. When they are unintended, are these offenses sins? Do we accept the view of the courts that ignorance of the law is no excuse? The Bible seems to say so about God's law, that a person may "know" inwardly without realizing it is a Divine law (Romans 2: 15).

In our Gospel reading this morning we heard Jesus tell Peter to forgive seventy times seven times. Presumably this meant forgiving the same person that many times. Perhaps it meant for the same offense committed that many times. Matthew places right after this a parable of Jesus that reveals the predicament we all face. Having been forgiven does not necessarily mean we will remember and forgive the one who offends us, perhaps even for a lesser offense than the one for which we were forgiven.

Perhaps this has something to do with the inability of "righteous people" to forgive. It seems inappropriate to forgive an offense intentionally offered to us. "How dare they think they will get away with this!" We so easily feel outraged at offenses done to us.

I think that there are some folk who imagine that it is sin itself that fascinates at least some in my trade most, rather than forgiveness of sin.

This past week I had a long chat in my living room with an older gentleman from Crieff, a town in Perthshire, Scotland, who told me with a merry twinkle in his eyes how his "hellfire and damnation" preacher made some errors which it was his duty to call to his attention. Let me be clear that the story he told me was funny, and he obviously loved his pastor dearly. He told the story for my sake because of the trade I'm in. But listening to him speak of his pastor made me wonder what kind of amusing anecdotes some folk in my own congregation might have to tell of their pastor for the amusement of some other pastor when they are traveling in Scotland!

The words "sin and guilt" get us all edgy, don't they? But today we're only to think of sin incidentally because it is the forgiveness of sin that is before us. But if we do not believe that sin is a reality, to speak of its forgiveness is pointless.

In the weeks leading up to this winter's Olympic Games the world has watched the miserable story unfold of the attempt by some people to physically impair one of the American ice skaters. The names are so well known to you I don't want to flash them before you again this morning. I was very touched to read Meg Greenfield's response to this sorry series of events. She wrote a wistful and wise column in this week's *Newsweek* magazine, in which she remarked:

"To me the key fact of the moral universe is the busted connection between what we say we think and what we evidently do think. Social critics complain these days—and with reason—that there has been a terrific revision downward, if not entirely into oblivion, of the idea of guilt. There is none, they say; there are only unfortunate conditions that compel bad things to happen. . .We aren't yet through with or rid of the old moral scheme of things, but we are, somehow, part way to a different one more sophisticated, some would say, and others, more permissive and corrupt.

Many folks would like to think we're better off without the preacher's words "sin" and "guilt," but with them gone, we're caught in a bind. First, what then do we call this terrible propensity that seems to be in us all that is botching up everything? Second, what can we do about it?"

We've tried hard to erase the bad feelings people get when they think in terms of the "old moral scheme," but they won't go away. Carl

Menninger asked from the vantage point of a psychiatrist, watching the behavior problems and anxieties of many average Americans pour out over some broken dam before him and his staff, **Whatever Became of Sin?** He concluded that very many people who came for therapy really needed forgiveness. Their problem was sin. Therapy has nothing to offer sin.

The multiplication of psychiatrists and counselors has not helped solve the problem when the "preacher's word sin" was eliminated. When our saintly forbears put into the Creed. "I believe in the forgiveness of sins," they were offering us a truth in which to rejoice. Sin can be forgiven. Not erased but forgiven. Not necessarily forgotten but forgiven. This terrible abrasive in the gears of Society has an antidote. The tragic flaw, which is in all of us, that takes away peace of mind, that makes peace in society impossible, and that eliminates any sense of peace within us or with God, has a cure. The cure is called "forgiveness of sin."

But what do we mean in speaking of this forgiveness? Whose forgiveness are we saying we believe in? Are we merely saying we believe God is going to do His job of forgiving, that is the counterpart to our tendency to sin? In this case, it would seem to take away all onus from sinning. As Paul asked, we can ask, "If grace much more abounds where there is sin, shouldn't we continue in sin that grace may abound?" If this is so, to say we believe in the forgiveness of sin simply moves us to carelessness in life. It is to teach us, "It doesn't matter what you do because God forgives every sin anyway—it's His job."

Together we say, "I believe in the forgiveness of sins." Remember what you believe—that you believe in forgiving others, and that you gratefully believe God forgives you. Paradoxically, we sometimes imagine we are being most true to God by refusing to forgive— which are the times we are acting least like God—whose mercy is everlasting. Our zeal for God's law may blind us to God's ways. Of course, the sins against you and me are real, as real as our sins against others and against God. But because there is forgiveness as the antidote to all this sin, let us receive it and give it gladly. Thanks be to God that in Jesus we are forgiven.

Let us pray: Lord God, thank you that your mercy is from everlasting to everlasting on those that honor you. Thank you that you have given to us of your nature. Now give us the grace to desire that part of your nature which we most need to receive. Grant to us the grace to forgive others, as we bask in the certainty that you have forgiven us, for Jesus sake, Amen.

I Believe in the Resurrection of the Body
Daniel 12:1-13; I Corinthians 15:12-26

One month from today we will be celebrating Easter. This sanctuary will be full of people looking forward to hearing again of Jesus' resurrection, singing the exuberant hymns, and of course, for the children the Easter egg hunt. Jesus' resurrection from the grave is the event in history that is the anchor of our faith. "If Christ be not raised," Paul wrote, "our faith is in vain" (**I Corinthians 15: 14**).

But today, though I am preaching on the resurrection, it is not His resurrection, but yours and mine that I have in mind. In the Apostles' Creed, the first time the resurrection is talked about, it is Jesus' body that is escaping the tomb. The second time the resurrection is mentioned, it is your body and mine that is escaping the tomb.

Though we often speak about Jesus' resurrection during life, the only time preachers usually talk about our bodies' resurrection is at funerals. Then, it sometimes seems to me, we talk about the resurrection of our bodies a bit wistfully, as though we're taking a final pot-shot, not too vigorously or confidently, at this inexplicable enemy that wins over the strongest of us—death. The grim reaper seems to stand rather confidently beside us then, quoting John Donne's poem: "don't ask to know for whom the bell tolls, it tolls for thee."

Dr. Sherwin Nuland—who is a medical doctor—has a lot of people reading his book *How We Die: Reflections on Life's Final Chapter*, nowadays. Since he is a physician, the things he says in this book are particularly interesting to people in my profession who perhaps see more often than others, other than nurses and doctors, the grim spectacle of people near the end of life. Far too often death looks indeed like a "grim reaper," as folk are tangled up in the web of wires and tubes, which are the final weapons human technology throws at death. They are the implements of the final desperate attempt to stave off what we all know awaits every one of us on this planet.

George Will, with characteristic panache, wrote: "Medicine has a job to do, but nature does too, and will do it. Nature's job is to send us packing so that subsequent generations can flourish."

There are some people who believe that the only way we live again after death is through these subsequent generations. The only life beyond death, they say, is our contribution to the pool of genes, or our good deeds about which people speak, or the good laws we make, or the beautiful buildings we build, or the great art we leave, or the books we write . . . These are how we "live again." The body, once dead, doesn't come alive again, but our influence remains alive.

The Bible makes clear, however, that there is more to our resurrection than this. Today I want to ponder the two aspects of the resurrection of our bodies that the Bible declares will take place. First, how the body comes alive again; second, what second, happens to that risen body.

How will the body become alive again? That the question should be asked places a premium on the body; it is not, in the end, disposable. Paul asks this question in I Corinthians 15: 35: "But someone will ask, 'How are the dead raised? With what kind of body do they come?'" His answer uses an analogy people in Indiana should understand well.

Every year I watch from my office window here at Faith the unfolding of this analogy of our resurrection. Each spring farmers plant in the fields around the church little soy beans and kernels of corn. When they plant the seed, they are confident that soon something will come up that doesn't look very much like what was planted.

Since many of our farmers have studied agriculture at Purdue, they understand the process whereby the dry little soy bean they planted splits open under the ground and sends up and down tiny shoots that are the first hints of roots and stem. They expect that what comes up will not look at all like the little seed they planted. The seed was dry and hard; the plant is full of moisture and tender. As the weeks and months of summer pass, that wizened little seed will have turned into a two-foot tall plant covered with bean pods. What was planted dry, hard, and evidently dead, came up alive!

Furthermore, even the farmer's youngest child knows before long that when soy beans are planted, soy beans will appear rather than Christmas trees. When kernels of corn are planted, God won't get confused and make turnips sprout from them. As Paul writes, "God gives to each kind of seed its own body" (I Cor. 15:38).

All of this is an analogy of how it is going to be for your bodies and mine. When we die, we are planted in the ground. In the ground because "we have this treasure in earthen vessels." Some die old and weak while some die young, but young or old, we are earthen vessels. This earth in which we live is not trash.

For some reason in our culture we plant these "people seeds" in expensive coffins and put the coffins in concrete boxes, separating them as far as possible from the dust from which they came. But this attempt to abort God's plan for our harvest won't have any effect on the outcome. (Or perhaps we should wonder what I Corinthians 15 would have told us if bodies in Paul's day had been so insulated from earth when they were buried.)

I Thessalonians 4:16-17 tells us how the moment of resurrection will happen. "The Lord himself will descend from heaven with a cry of command, with the archangel's call, and with the sound of the trumpet of God. And the dead in Christ will rise first; then we who are alive, who are left, shall be caught up together with them in the clouds to meet the Lord in the air; and so, we shall always be with the Lord. So, comfort one another with these words." To refer to our "earthly bodies," is not to say we have them only on earth, but that they are made of earth.

Here Paul elaborates on what Jesus taught: "[God] will send his angels with a great sound of a trumpet, and they shall gather together his elect from the four winds, from one end of heaven to the other" (Matt. 24:31).

There are a lot of details, of course, that nobody knows about. We read the word "elect," and we wonder if this means "elect" in the sense that Calvin taught. Double election to grace or condemnation, so that does Matthew 24: 31 refer only to the elect to God's favor? The others' destiny is too fearful to mention?

Whatever that may be, we could visualize the picture better if everyone were neatly buried in a church graveyard, so that at the resurrection, all the old-fashioned churches with picturesque graveyards would spring to life, with all the old saints rising from their tombs, maybe not even disrupting the soil on the way up—just as Jesus passed through walls after His resurrection.

But what of the martyrs who were burned at the stake, or what about people buried at sea, or eaten up by man-eating tigers? I think these questions all hinge on our assumption that when the Bible talks about bodies rising, it does mean bodies that will rise. The Book of Revelation tells us that at the first resurrection the sea gives up its dead (20:13). If God can get the dead out of the sea, I suspect He'll have little trouble retrieving those who have turned to ashes. If you're wondering how risen babies or risen elderly folk will look—remember that a mature corn stalk doesn't look like the kernel that was planted. We shall be changed!

Our bodies are not beside the point. Of course, we know that while we are alive. That's why moisturizing creams sell so well, and Nordic tracks, and Carter's little liver pills; that's why tanning salons can succeed in selling the illusion of health, even though we know that tanning is not very good for the skin. That's why we buy "life insurance," even though we know this isn't insurance for life at all, but only a euphemism for a way to make our relatives a bit less sad when we die.

The importance of the body goes beyond the importance we usually think about. As Scripture says, "Do you not know that your bodies are members of Christ? Do you not know that your body is the temple of the Holy Spirit" (I Cor. 6:15, 19)? I'm tempted to say that God doesn't have a "Spiritual" enterprise with us. The Hebrew Bible has a word for everything that is us—nephesh. There are not three parts, but as we try to understand the Trinity as "three persons, one essence," so we too are one essence, though we think of categories of our composition: body, soul, and spirit. It is our idea, not taught by Scripture, that I know of. The reason why we should avoid the sins of the body—sexual sins, but also the sins of persistent over-eating, of over-drinking, of over-working, of becoming couch potatoes, failing to take proper care of our bodies through exercise and rest—is that our entire bodies are very much a part of God's enterprise with us. Our bodies were God's idea, and "they are fearfully and wonderfully made." Heaven, I have the hunch, will be populated with bodies, that is, people. It will not be populated with shadowy, saintly ghosts. Which probably means the picture of heaven as fluffy clouds on which the saints sit strumming little Irish harps makes for a cute picture, that's all. I picture heaven as being the fulfillment of God's original idea of earth, the one He once called good. Heaven then as Genesis tells of it was the sky.

Extrapolations from a later idea of heaven resulted in Augustine's question, "Are we to understand by that expression, *heaven and earth*, all that God made is to be included and brought to mind first in a general way, and that then the manner of creation is to be worked out in detail . . ." ([**The Literal Meaning of Genesis**, two volumes, New York, Newman Press, 1982] I, 3, 22). So that when God created heaven, he created all that are there, including angels, that were worked out in detail later. All this though Genesis only tells us that God made the earth and sky. Genesis tells us that God's creation of earth and sky was in a sequence that concluded with the creation of Adam in His image and likeness. The details would come later.

Speaking of heaven. that gets us to the second question about the resurrection. What will happen to these raised bodies of ours if the people involved were notoriously bad—like Hitler?

In the prophet Daniel we learn that when people are raised after death. for some it will be everlasting life, and for others shame and everlasting contempt (12:2). Immediately the prophet accentuates the joyous part of the story: "And those who are wise shall shine like the brightness of the firmament. and those who turn many to righteousness, like the stars for ever and ever." Heaven will be wonderful beyond our dreams. Every joy you and I know now is only like a shadow of heaven.

But there is that other part of the story I dare not ignore. There is a heaven, we are told, but there is also hell. Hell is not a hot topic these days. Pardon the pun. Or perhaps I should say, it's "too hot to handle." A popular book a pastor wrote proposes instead, **Love Wins**.

Before attempting to offer something about the "hot topic," it is good to remember that several not-English words are translated "hell." So "hell" in the Bible, particularly in an old translation like the KJV doesn't always refer to the place engulfed in unquenchable flames.

In the Hebrew Bible one word is used thirty-one times, *sheol*, that meant only the place of the dead, as in Psalm 16: 10, "Thou wilt not leave my soul in hell." In the New Testament there are three words translated hell, *Hades*, as in Matthew 16: 18, "I will build my church and the gates of hell shall not prevail against it." *Hades* was like *Sheol*. The hot place in the New Testament is *Gehinna*. This word gets its name from the Valley of Hinnom outside Jerusalem where refuse was burned. In the movie, "Ben Hur," Ben Hur's mother and sister are doomed to live in that horrible place because they are lepers. This word is used twelve times in the New Testament.

Jesus uses this last word eleven times in Matthew and Luke. The Epistle of James uses it once. Then there is the term "outer darkness," another image of a fearful destiny. First, in Mathew 8: 12, after healing a Roman centurion's servant in Capernaum, Jesus said, "many will come from east and west and sit at table with Abraham, Isaac, and Jacob in the kingdom of heaven," he says, "while the sons of the kingdom will be thrown into the outer darkness; there men will weep and gnash their teeth." This fearful phrase appears four times more in Matthew. The term is also found in Luke 13: 28 in Jesus fearful parable of the narrow and wide gates. Those who try to enter the wide gate, hoping for salvation, will hear the words," I do not know where you come from; depart from me, all you workers of iniquity! There you will weep and gnash your teeth."

Jesus speaks of "eternal fire" and "eternal damnation," as well as of "eternal life."

Throughout the Bible there are reminders that God is a righteous judge—which means God is fair and honest. As we read in Ecclesiastes 12:14: "God shall bring every work into judgment, with every secret thing, whether it be good or whether it be evil."

Daniel described this scene of judgment: "I beheld till the thrones were cast down and the Ancient of days did sit. whose garment was white as snow, and the hair of his head like the pure wool: his throne was like the fiery flame, and his wheels as burning fire. A fiery stream issued and came forth from before him: thousands ministered to him, and ten thousand times ten thousand stood before him: the judgment was set, and the books were opened" (7:9-10).

Jesus spoke often of this judgment. He said. "Every idle word that men shall speak, they shall give account thereof in the day of judgment" (Matt. 12:36). He taught that the world was like a field a farmer plants in which there is wheat, but there are also weeds. Referring to the judgment, Jesus said: "In the time of harvest I will say to the reapers, gather together first the weeds, and bind them in bundles to burn them; but gather the wheat into my barn" (Matt. 13:30). Jesus said, "There is nothing hid, which shall not be manifested" (Mark 4:22). I could go on and on quoting Jesus about the fact that in the judgment that comes at the end of time, we will discover that we have been responsible during this life for what we do.

The Book of Revelation tells us of a "great white throne" on which there will sit someone of such majesty that heaven and earth tremble before Him. John writes:

"I saw the dead, small and great, stand before God; and the books were opened: and another book was opened, which is the book of life: and the dead were judged out of those things which were written in the books, according to their works" (20:12).

The Bible is not as sparing as we are nowadays in reminding us that God will not hesitate to condemn those who are guilty before Him.

It speaks not only of heaven, but also of hell. Hell was created for the devil and his angels (Matthew 25: 14). But not only for them.

Paul, who taught us most of what we know about God's grace, also taught us "God is not deceived. Whatever a man sows that will he also reap. For he that sows to the flesh shall of the flesh reap corruption; but he that sows to the Spirit shall of the Spirit reap life everlasting" (Gal. 6:8). In brief, it matters how we live!

What does all this mean? To ignore it is to ignore part of Holy Scripture. We have learned things about this fearful aspect of the Good News from many favorite writers, but we <u>know</u> very little; what we know and what we have learned are two different things.

Extreme Calvinists emphasize an idea of double-election derived from Paul's teaching about Esau and Jacob in Romans 9: 11, "though they were not yet born and had done nothing either good or bad, in order that God's purpose of election might continue, not because of works but because of his call . . ."

But I wonder how this verse settles beside Paul's statement two chapters later, "For God has consigned all men to disobedience, that he may have mercy on all" (Romans 11: 32). The former proof text leaves no one with hope because what person can know whether she is of the elect, no matter how firmly she may be convinced that she is. The latter proof-text, coming at the close of Paul's extended argument through eleven chapters, of the ways of God, gives everyone hope. If "all" means "all," then "all" will receive mercy. I have heard the explanation from a Calvinist friend that the "all" only refers to the "elect."

I have noted earlier in this study that from the Old Testament to the New Testament there is development of some key ideas.

Whereas Exodus 20: 4-6, tells us that God remembers until the fourth generation after those who made for themselves a graven image, they would be punished for the sin of the forebears. I don't know what to make of the qualifying phrase, "of those who hated me." But it seems to mean that despite later generations turning away from idols, they are held accountable for the idolatry of their forebears, three or four generations earlier. The following phrase is a bit more cheerful, "showing steadfast love to thousands of those who love me and keep my commandments." There are far fewer heirs of the idolaters than of the ones who did not bow to a graven image.

Jeremiah 31: 30 tells us that God changed this retribution on the generations of an idolater's family. Now, "everyone shall die for his own sin." The other prophet of the exile, Ezekiel expands on this. Ezekiel 18 is devoted to an elaboration of this change in God's ways with people.

The progress continues in the Gospel of John where Jesus dies for the sins of the world. The promise of salvation is extended to "whosoever," which means, everyone. While John also writes of the necessity of belief, the promise has no boundaries.

I wonder if Paul's sweeping statement in Romans 11: 32 is the final New Testament teaching on which to focus. The Gospels have some fearful teachings but are we to see that as the teachings of Christ matured in the understanding of the Apostle Paul, he concluded that while nobody's good works could secure for them eternal life, God's mercy could and would fill the gap between a person's lack of deserving and the goal of being welcomed into eternal life.

But let me not end only with this warning; with the very real warning comes very real reason for hope. If God gave us what we deserve, none of us would end up in heaven. If you are honest with yourself, you know this is true of you, as I know it is true of me. But the Gospel is brimming with the Good News that God offers us forgiveness of sin and the promise of eternal life through Jesus Christ.

Here's what to do to receive God's good plan for your body after it is raised from death. While you are living now, respond to Jesus' invitation, "Come to me."

Following Jesus is not an inexpensive insurance policy to get out of hell. It means believing first that He welcomes you and forgives you. Usually people come to Jesus because they recognize they are tired and heavy laden, but now welcome to a place where they can find rest. To this weariness Jesus offers rest. So, ask for this forgiveness; ask for this rest.

Second, coming to Jesus means becoming His disciple—that is, accepting the discipline of Jesus' way of life. If you come to Jesus wanting rest, but not wanting to be His disciple, well, I'm not sure what that means, ultimately. Jesus spoke a stern word recorded in the Gospel of Matthew 7: 21-23, "Not everyone who says to me, 'Lord, Lord' shall enter the kingdom of heaven, but he who does the will of my Father who is in heaven." This is followed by one of those frightening statements, "On that day many will say to me, 'did we not prophesy in your name, and cast out demons in your name, and do many mighty works in your name?' And then will I declare to them, 'I never knew you; depart from me, you evildoers'."

Coming up with a conclusion from these various and varying passages in the New Testament falls this way and that among those that consult the New Testament as the basis of their doctrines. I'm tempted to say that we have been purposely kept on edge on ultimate things.

When I was nineteen and had just determined to be a Christian "for real," after growing up in a missionary home and feeling like a wash out in terms of taking part in what Christianity really was, I wrote to C.S. Lewis, asking him what the objective of the junior devil in was tempting the Christian in his little book, **The Screwtape Letters**. Was the goal to tempt Christians to make them fall and lose their salvation? Or was the purpose just for the devilish delight in seeing a Christian fall? The great man replied to this young lad's letter in a hand-written letter, using a dip pen, with corrections in pencil here and there. He proposed that God presents two ideas in the variety of the New Testament's teaching. For those apt to be self-confident God has the New Testament writers write fearful things lest they become presumptuous. For those that are timid, and easily discouraged when they fall, He gives an opposite message. "No one and nothing can pluck you out of my hand."

Whether this is on target or not we'll all discover much later, but I found this explanation of the purpose of the Bible's various sometimes conflicting teachings reassuring. It's all intentional. It's not a matter of "contradictions."

Jesus doesn't invite you and me to Him to keep carrying all the baggage that made us weary to begin with. Leave your familiar sins behind; they are a heavy burden. Leave your pride, your greed for things, your self-destroying appetites, your hatreds behind. Replace them with Jesus' yoke, which is light.

It has been well said that "at the heart of Christianity lies a holy dread." "The fear of the Lord is the beginning of wisdom," the Bible says. This fear has to do with recognizing that God is a righteous judge who will treat us fairly; He will give us what we deserve. The hope of the Christian message is this—When we hide ourselves in Jesus, accepting Him and His life, then God sees Jesus when He looks at us.

This morning I want to say very clearly to each of us, we never need fear what will happen to our bodies after we die, because God has offered us this wonderful plan, which though we cannot begin to understand it, we can tell it's good news. God will not force it on you, but He offers it to you. Believe it; receive it; and you will enjoy life—in your body—forever. Reject it, and, well, we must let God take care of that option.

This morning, as we come to the Lord's Table, I invite you to come, not only to receive the elements of bread and wine you see, but to realize that as physically as possible, here the Lord Jesus offers Himself to you. Receive Him with a thankful heart, then see what follows.

Let us pray: O Lord how to speak of things so beyond us all. Grant that whatever that is right and true of what we have thought, may refresh us and ignite in us the Gospel life. Amen.

I Believe in the Life Everlasting
Psalm 133; John 3:1-17

I know that today Purdue plays its final home game, that today our hoopsters can grab first place in the Big Ten all by themselves, and that this game begins at 12:30. I am a bit daunted to know that my topic this morning has to do with "everlasting life," which surely must take an awful long time to explain. But many years' experience has softened my idealism. I will try to be more suggestive than exhaustive.

Today we have arrived at the final statement of the Apostles' Creed. We begin the Creed expressing our belief in God, who existed before He created anything, and we end expressing our belief not only in God's continuing existence, but also in ours.

We might say that at the end we declare our confidence that finally our lives will merge not into God, as the pantheists suggest, but into God's kind of life in whose image we were made. This doesn't mean that we will become "one with God," in the way the Eastern mystics talk about unity with God. When they talk about unity with God, they mean merging into the Godhead in such a way that there is no distinction between people and God. The Bible never tells us to expect that to happen.

But it does mean that as we call God "the eternal God," we can look on our lives as eternal too; we are, in Christ, eternal people.

There are differences between us and God, of course, and always will be. His life had no beginning and ours does. We'll remember this, I suspect, if we think about such things, in eternity. Also, God is perfect in holiness while we are defective even in that shadowy way our goodness reflects His holiness. We will carry in our resurrection body the scars of our flawed life here on earth., When we say I believe in life everlasting, are we essentially pointing to the endless time when we will fulfill Jesus' command: "Be perfect as your father in heaven is perfect?" We have entered a process of change now that will end with us looking like Jesus; "We will be like Him, for we shall see Him as He is" (I John 3:2). Paul, in fact, referred to this as a metamorphosis (II Corinthians 3:18), the very word we use to describe how a not very attractive caterpillar changes into a beautiful butterfly. "And we all, with unveiled face, beholding the glory of the Lord, are being changed into his likeness from one degree of glory to another; for this comes from the Lord who is the Spirit."

The reference to "unveiled face," Paul drew from a somewhat "spooky" time in Moses' life after he came down from the mountain, and then when he entered the tent of meeting to speak with God. Exodus 34; 30, 33, "And when Aaron and all the people of Israel saw Moses, behold, the skin of his face shone, and they were afraid to come near him . . . He put a veil on his face; but whenever Moses went in before the Lord to speak with him, he took the veil off . . . the people of Israel saw the face of Moses, that the skin of Moses' face shone; and Moses would put the veil upon his face again, until he went in to speak with him." Paul used this incident in Moses' life as the metaphor to describe the incandescence, so to speak, of the life of one in whom the Spirit of God lives. This Spirit of God comes to a person who is part of the "dispensation of the Spirit" (3: 8), that is, I believe, to the one who has become a follower of Christ.

It is good to remember that our word "everlasting" comes from the word that also means "eternal." "Eternal" has overtones that go much beyond time and refer to quality of life too.

It is this quality of life about which I want to speak this morning because I think that this is what Jesus longed to see begin in people who come to Him in faith. I believe that usually our thinking about eternal life chases a red herring—the idea that it is a way of living that only comes after death, because we are wary of "mystical" thinking and convinced that all this about salvation is straight-forward and has to do with our bodies. That is, unless we are hung up on some idea of our "souls" being saved, and the body, that St. Francis called "brother ass," is not part of the equation in salvation.

I am convinced that unless we think of eternal life as a quality of life that we are to go after now, we short-change ourselves. I realize that we are "God's workmanship," as Paul once put it (Ephesians 2:10), but we are also "disciples," which means people who have entered the discipline of following Jesus. This deliberate, often difficult, life of following Jesus, is the way you and I are to experience eternal life now. Indeed, if we are involved in the process, expecting to see good results, "growth in grace" from following Jesus NOW, every good development will remind us that indeed it is due to God's new impulse at work in us. This new life IS eternal life already. Every improvement in us is a reminder of the fact that we have eternal life.

In the conversation with Nicodemas that I read for you a few moments ago, Jesus told this good man that nobody can see the Kingdom of God unless he is "born anew," or "born again," as we usually use the term. "Unless one is born of water and the Spirit, he cannot enter the kingdom of God." It seems that Jesus here referred to natural birth by water as the way we enter human life, and the second birth by the Holy Spirit as the way we enter eternal life. Both happen in this life.

John explained to us in the first chapter that those who believe in Jesus receive the power to become children of God. They weren't God's children in this unique sense naturally. This is a birth "not of bloods" we read in John 1:13, nor of the will of the flesh, nor of the will of man, but of God. Our translations customarily translate the term, "not of bloods," as "not of blood." I think "bloods" refers to the mingling of the mother and father's "DNA" in a baby's body. This mingling of bloods is different from the "new birth." The heredity of being "born from above," is different from our human heredity.

When we believe in Jesus, we are born with "God's seed" in us (I John 3:9).[1] This is about as vivid a way as possible of expressing our new birth when we believe in Jesus. It borrows on the human physiology of birth where each zygote has the seed of the father as well as the ovum of the mother. Now eternal life, the new life, God's kind of life begins, much as human life began when we were born, or conceived, physically. So, we can expect characteristics of "eternal life" to appear, just as new born babies show characteristics of

---

[1] I John 3:9 reads that God's seed (*sperma* - from which we get our word sperm) remains in the one who has been born of God.

human life—hunger, personality, cooing, tears, etc. Eternal life has characteristics too.

I wonder if you can point to a time in your life when you know this new thing began. Not everyone can, I know, because there are some fortunate folk who learned of Jesus early in life and cannot think of a time when they did not believe in Jesus. But for all of us, for those who can point to the moment, as I can, or who cannot remember a time when they did not believe in Jesus, the new eternal life is to be a different life from the ordinary life.

I think of the description of the beginning of Christian's life in Bunyan's *Pilgrim's Progress*. He saw that the highway up which he had to go had a fence on both sides called "Salvation." This highway between the walls of Salvation involved a steep climb that was hard for him because on his back he had this heavy burden. But he came to an upward slope where he saw a Cross below which he saw a sepulcher. Bunyan writes: "I saw in my dream, that just as Christian came up with the Cross, his burden loosed from off his shoulders, and fell from his back, and began to tumble, and so continued to do, till it came to the mouth of the sepulcher, where it fell in, and I saw it no more." He was given a new coat to wear.

The heavy burden, of course, was the burden of all that afflicts us in this life, our sin, our cares—the memory of it, the habit of it, and the discomfort of it. This burden fell into Jesus' grave and disappeared. The new coat was Jesus' righteousness that replaced his heavy burden. He felt free and light on his feet.

Bunyan's allegory here is beautifully on target. We begin this new life with shedding the heavy burden of our past. When we baptize our little ones, we begin this new life for them, promising to give them direction in the way of Jesus. They, with their parents are "new creations;" the old has passed away. But what is the life beyond this wonderful entrance into eternal life? I'm not wise enough nor have we time enough for me to be very expansive in describing it. How many of us, after our baptism either as babies or as adults, find that after that our way of life doesn't always look like a "new life in Christ." Happily, this is part of what we see "darkly," as Paul put it in I Corinthians 13. God does not see us darkly.

The Old Testament reading this morning describes one aspect of this new life wonderfully. Perhaps this aspect is described because it reflects an outlook that is the precondition to many of the other aspects of eternal life we look for. The 133rd Psalm has its theme unity among brothers, a theme that we delight in when we see it happen but are somehow predisposed to be wary of it nowadays. I digress to suggest that our democratic Christianity is hide bound to cling to our uniqueness in understanding of the Christian way.

The illustrations the psalmist uses are from a moment in the life of Moses and his brother, Aaron, and from a beautiful place in Israel where a pure cap of snow lingers through much of the year, the twin peaks of Mt. Hermon.

At the end of the psalm the psalmist says that unity between brothers is the life-situation where God has commanded the blessing of eternal life.

Look at how he explains this unity of heart between brothers. It is pictured in the moment Moses anointed Aaron to be the first High Priest of ancient Israel. When Moses anointed Aaron, it was a bit like the way I baptize folk here at Faith Church: the oil ran over Aaron's head, down onto his beard, and onto the collar of his robe. It was a generous out-pouring of oil; no mere token dab of oil to fulfill the minimal duty of applying oil in the rite of anointing for sacred office.

What made this more noticeable was that, at least as the Jews have long understood it, Moses wanted to be the priest. He didn't want to confer this office on his brother. Josephus tells us that Moses addressed the people of Israel, telling them that he wanted to be the priest, but that God had chosen Aaron—oddly enough—because of his brother's virtues—that is, his own. Josephus was not alone in telling this little detail. If Moses indeed wanted to be High Priest, and had to confer it on his brother instead, the picture of him anointing Aaron so generously suggests that he had swallowed his pride, and fully accepted his brother as High Priest. Selfishness was replaced with a generous heart. Envy was buried. So that this anointing of Aaron was a beautiful act like the falling of dew on Mt. Hermon. The anointing was not with a drop of oil, but with a pitcher full.

Here, the psalmist writes, here in this setting of unity between brothers, where there was reason to be jealousy and hostility, is where God offers the blessing of eternal life. This is how eternal life looks.

Do you remember how Jesus said His followers would be recognized? "By this will all people know that you are my disciples, that you love one another." Jesus described a recognizable love, a quality of interaction in which each seeks the good of the other, rather than her own good. It is a quality of life together that is described on the community level, what deep affection looks like between people. It is as far as possible from the self-seeking ways of society.

What would Faith Church look like if this were our guide to life together? Imagine yourself wanting something very much that could only be given to one person, and when you have the chance to claim it, you give it to someone else instead. When this outlook starts to take place in your mind and in mine, we are beginning to see what eternal life looks like.

Paul told us that the things that are seen are temporal, which means, "only for a while."

The things that are unseen are eternal. Eternal life, we might say, is made up of things that are hardly seen—people living together wanting to give to one another what otherwise they would claim for themselves. Imagine this describing your outlook on life—and mine. Imagine seeing this, so that Paul's saying is undone, and we can see unseen things—eternal life replacing self-centered life. There, the psalmist writes, is life forevermore—eternal life—God's kind of life.

I lift this life before you—children, young people, and those of the rest of us who clutch after a life in which peace seems so elusive. We say, "I believe in the life everlasting." If we believe in eternal life, let us grasp its ways now.

Perhaps C.S. Lewis was right. Maybe the way we are in the hereafter will extend into eternity aspects of how we were this side of death. I think that Christians who choose to be morose, or greedy, or selfish, or brash, or grumbling on this side of death, will probably show some scars in eternity. Some of us will have crowns given to us to lay at Jesus' feet that will have more stars ornamenting them than others.

We love to sing: that wonderful medieval hymn, still pertinent today, "Jesus, our only joy be Thou, As Thou our prize wilt be, Jesus, be thou our glory now, and through eternity." So, may it be.

Let us pray: We bless You Lord God, that you have not only placed within us a profound longing for unending life, but You have created us with a longing for a good life—filled with peace, joy, goodness, and love. Our restless spirits yearn for you. We acknowledge that unless You give us unsparingly of Your Holy Spirit, our yearning can never be satisfied. As you have drawn us to Yourself by Your Holy Spirit, so fill us with Your Holy Spirit, that in this life we may enjoy a clear foretaste of the blessed life. And grant that we may show this way of life to those who do not know the Lord Jesus, that they may see our good works, glorify You, and be drawn to eternal life as well. This is your plan; and it is our request. For Jesus'

www.ingramcontent.com/pod-product-compliance
Lightning Source LLC
Chambersburg PA
CBHW071913110526
44591CB00011B/1669